Joy in Stone

THE CATHEDRAL OF REIMS

By Sabra Holbrook

Sir Tristan of All Time
A Stranger in My Land
Joy in Stone: The Cathedral
of Reims

JOY IN STONE
The Cathedral of Reims

Sabra Holbrook
illustrated by Herbert Danska

⚜

Farrar, Straus and Giroux
New York

For
LEIF
who I hope is also laughing for joy

Contents

"Je suis toute l'histoire de France. Je *suis* la France."
I am all the history of France. I *am* France.

R. Burnard: *Sept Siècles d'Histoire devant la Cathédrale*

BY WAY OF BEGINNING

Many people think of a church as a building. But buildings don't build themselves. People build them. A church may *have* buildings. A church *is* people.

This book is about people who built and rebuilt a cathedral over a period of fifteen hundred years. It is the story of how that cathedral became the soul of a nation and how it adapted to changing times from the days of tribal kings to the present.

A few of the builders were saints and some were sinners, but most were a human mixture of both. Kings and peasants, priests and politicians, sculptors and stonecutters, stained-glass artisans, architects, beggars, prostitutes, guilds of merchants, troupes of actors, soldiers and peacemakers, poets and historians—legion are the ranks who, in one way or another, at one time or another, have helped nurture the cathedral. And each succeeding generation has also been nurtured by the gifts of earlier ones. In this ongoing giving and receiving not even the dead are dead.

For the intimacy of my exposure to the cathedral of Reims I should like to thank the French Commissariats Généraux au Tourisme in Paris, Reims, and New York. I owe special debts of gratitude to Monsignor Berton, formerly the Archbishop of Reims; to Mlle Bénédicte Sermonne, a hostess of Reims's Office de Tourisme; and to a young priest who prefers not to be mentioned by name, whose sermon on love and joy is quoted in Chapter I. I wish also to acknowledge with appreciation the informative interviews granted me by M. Pomarède, Conservateur des Musées de Reims, and M. André, Architecte des Bâtiments de France.

Sabra Holbrook

I

A Cathedral Is Born

M*erci.*" The girl in the yellow pants suit murmurs her thanks with a smile as a man drops his Sunday offering into the basin she is passing down one side of the cathedral's center aisle. On the opposite side a boy in blue jeans grins and nods his thanks as his basin fills. Acknowledgment of every single gift is the custom in the cathedral of Reims, France.

As the pair moves along, organ music storms the pinnacles of the Gothic arches supporting the roof more than a hundred feet above. The girl hums the melody. The boy marks the beat with his head. Like many of the other young people who make up half of the three hundred or so worshippers this morning, these two are music lovers. Time and again the cathedral draws them with the quality of its music.

They have come for an early service, timed to free them for their customary Sunday pursuits: picnicking, fishing, hunting, boating, clambering through castle ruins, hiking forest trails. The final Amen will barely echo through the vast cathedral before they reach cars prepacked for excursions. Tiny compacts shaped like hunchbacked beetles have been loaded with an incredible amount of gear, from picnic lunches and folding tables and chairs to frog nets, guns, and fishing rods, and, in winter, skis. Off to the country!

"Our enemy is the automobile," lamented a recent archbishop of Reims. But his eyes crinkled with satisfaction as he added, "So we have found ways to outwit it. More services." An evening service is timed for the hour of return from Sunday spreeing.

Morning or evening, the young members of the congregation come as they are. They have their styles, which suit them well. The boys are trim-bearded. Their hair falls midway between chin and shoulders. Their jeans are low-slung, bell-bottomed, well pressed; the belts are wide, copper-buckled. If there is a chill in the air, a vented corduroy jacket, flared from the waist down, may be slung over one shoulder.

The girls are miniskirted or pants-suited, their long hair combed back from their faces and caught with a metal or leather barrette. Their coats are short and tightly belted, their long knitted shawls draped and redraped around their shoulders.

These are the youth fashions of the 1970's in the cathedral of Reims. The series of cathedrals and churches that have stood on this site have been the setting for all sorts of dress since the days when bishops baptized tribesmen who grew their hair to their waists and drooped their mustaches to their shoulders. The aisles where today's youth collect offerings have been swept by the ermine trains of kings about to be crowned at the altar. Down these same aisles the mailed feet of murderers have stalked their prey. The outsize black hat of Napoleon, Joan of Arc's banner embroidered with fleurs-de-lis, the white robes of saints, the sackcloth of repentant sinners, the smocks of peasants, the rags of beggars— all these have been seen in the procession of historical personages at Reims. The procession, fifteen centuries long, has rarely been tranquil. The stones of Reims have been sluiced, not merely with baptismal water, but with blood. Gutted by fires, all but leveled by bombs, a cathedral—restored and again restored—has survived. And with each re-creation its personality has emerged unchanged, laughing at affliction, defying disaster.

This invincible joy was the central theme of the fourteen architects who, through seven centuries, designed and directed the construction and reconstruction of the cathedral as it stands today. Although remnants of earlier buildings on the site remain in the crypt, the present cathedral is the product of work begun in the thirteenth century.

Of all the joyful faces carved by the sculptors whom the architects hired, the most famous belongs to a statue known as *"L'Ange au Sourire,"* the smiling angel. Congregations pass the statue as they enter or leave by the left-hand door of the main façade. Despite this angel's fame, however, it does not possess the most infectious of the cathedral's angelic smiles. That honor belongs to the archangel Gabriel. He stands to the right of the middle door of the front façade, in the act of announcing to Mary that God has chosen her to be the mother of Christ. Quite obviously he takes supreme delight in the news. Flesh fluted around the eyes, lips parted and upturned, he is on the verge of divine laughter. Since the year 1250 when a sculptor from Verdun named Nicolas carved him from a peach-colored block of limestone, Gabriel has survived with the cathedral through fires, wars, and revolutions, losing to time and violence only a right wing and part of his right arm.

The multitude of lesser angels distributed around the exterior join in a chorus of mirth. Even one who accompanies the statue of a freshly beheaded saint carrying his own head smiles as though to proclaim the bloody incident merely a momentary interruption in the saint's eternal career. Nor are the angels the only ones who have given themselves over to glee. The limestone lips of saints, kings, prophets also smile. Even the gargoyles grin. The fashion in the twelfth to fourteenth centuries, the great age of European cathedral building, was to place these gargoyles, grotesque caricatures of animals and humans, in high cornices and at the bases of spires. But the eagles, dogs and cats, deer, wild boar and foxes, cows and rams of Reims went fashion one better. They are different from the gargoyles of any other medieval cathedral. No caricatures they. Completely natural, they are frisky and well fed. The human faces, undistorted, seem to share a secret joke.

At Reims, all God's creation, from animal to archangel, seems to laugh with Him for the joy of the life He has created. Inevitably, the good humor is catching. The young people heading for their cars when the Sunday service is over are almost always smiling. Busloads of tourists who visit the cathedral smile back at the statues. "For those of us who work here," said the Archbishop who had triumphed over the automobile, "those smiles are the greatest reward. They are proof of the contagion of the cathedral's delight."

Sermons as well may reflect the cathedral's spirit. At the service where the yellow-suited girl and blue-jeaned boy were taking up the offering, a young priest preached on joy. "Not with dry hearts should we enter this cathedral," he warned. "Rather our hearts should overflow with the joy of having been created." His sermon was brief. The service was low-keyed, relaxed. The Bible was read in modern French. The singing was vigorous, with the Archbishop himself pacing back and forth in the sanctuary, waving his arms like a windmill to encourage the congregation to give their all and occasionally stepping down to the organist to suggest speeding the accompaniment.

To congregations who thronged the cathedral in cen-turies long gone, the modern informality of the Mass, that service which celebrates Christ's last supper with His dis-ciples, would no doubt seem strange. Gone are pomp and ceremony. The only departure from down-to-earth simplicity is the pageantry of the acolytes' performance. Eight boy acolytes, robed in red cassocks with white surplices, assist the priest and Archbishop. At the climax of the Mass they kneel, holding candles they have lighted from those which stand three feet high in three-foot-high golden candlesticks on the black and white marble altar. When the Archbishop comes down from the altar to distribute Communion, four acolytes accompany him, a pair on either side. In the rustle of their robes there seems to be a faint whisper of the past. Otherwise the service is of today.

It is one of many services, Sunday and every day, held for eleven thousand parishioners. The Archbishop is rightly proud that Reims is one of the largest, as well as one of the most stable, parishes in all France. For it is a parish church as well as a cathedral. The parish is family. The cathedral is history. Classified as a historic monument by the French government, Reims remains under the government's watchful eye. Its Fine Arts division provides a subsidy and supervisory personnel to see that the cathedral is kept in continuous repair and its medieval character maintained.

The Archbishop so proud of Reim's stability and even more proud of its joy is Monsignor Berton. His theories about church music are as dynamic as his leading of the hymns. *"Il faut faire chanter tout le monde,"* he insists. "We must make everyone sing." He believes strongly that too much church music has been written for choirs and too little for congregations. He wants worshippers to participate actively in all parts of a service, spoken or sung. "Church composers," he says, "must give us increasingly a repertory worthy of the service of God but equally appropriate for popular use. It is an injustice to God and man to reduce a congregation systematically to silence."

Monsignor Berton is one of a long line who have led— and who have yet to lead—Reims's clergy and people.* Meeting him at his time of leadership, one sees the ca-

* He retired and was succeeded in office in 1973.

thedral in a light which, partly its own, is also partly shed by its Archbishop. No new connection, this; cathedral and archbishop have almost always illumined each other.

You might come upon Monsignor Berton in his time, any day, wandering through any part of the building. You would not know he is the Archbishop. Thoroughly unpretentious, he wears no clerical garb, not even a reversed collar, except when officiating at a service. The only insignia of his rank and profession is a small pin in the shape of a cross on the lapel of his jacket. From the manner in which he pauses before this or that statue, the manner in which his eyes seek out the vaulted ceiling, the gentle brush his hand may give to a stone, the interest with which he regards visitors, you might detect his proprietary concern. Certainly you would think, This man loves this place. If your imagination is active, you might also think, This place loves this man.

How did this man come to this place? Not by ambition, not even by dedication. Purely by chance. In his teens he had reached a point in his education where he was supposed to move on with his classmates to the next grade, but according to law he was twenty-five days too young. To move on he would have to take a special exam. A friend attending a seminary in preparation for the priesthood said, "Why don't you come to the seminary? You won't need to take any exam and your age doesn't matter."

And that is what young Berton did. He himself tells the story as it was and concludes, "So you see, I can't claim any holy motives for entering the priesthood." His eyes twinkle behind his spectacles. He runs a hand through thinning white hair and adds, "My mother was horrified. But what she couldn't see, and of course neither did I at that time, was that commitment would come in the course of study. To my friend it did not come. He dropped out of the seminary; he became a banker. I might suspect that God, in His infinite wisdom, intended me to replace my friend in His service— if I didn't think the suspicion presumptuous."

By no means were all of the 155 archbishops and twenty-eight bishops who preceded Monsignor Berton committed solely, or even deeply, to the service of God and mankind. All through the Middle Ages, and up until relatively modern times, bishoprics and archbishoprics were posts prized for the political influence and material holdings that went with them. Three archbishops and two bishops were so blatant about their lust for power and wealth that they were deposed. Four of them were removed as a consequence of having allied themselves with what turned out to be the losing side in struggles between royal rivals for the throne of France. Had they picked a winner, they would no doubt have been rewarded instead of punished. One was banished for stealing from the King's treasury. Others, who operated more smoothly or subtly, got away with such practices.

Among the early founders of the cathedral there is no such record of rascality. Indeed, the earliest of these records, flavoring truth with legend, links the founders with Christ's disciple St. Peter. It maintains that fifty or sixty years after the death of Christ, saints whom the French call Sixte and Sinice, disciples of St. Peter, brought Christianity to Gallic tribes of pagan barbarians in the Reims area.

Another myth, which is nothing but myth, proclaims that the town of Reims to which the two saints came had been founded by Romulus and Remus, a pair of Roman brothers brought up by wolves. The story goes that the two brothers stood on separate hilltops waiting for a sign from the heavens to show which one should claim the territory. Remus saw six vultures. Then Romulus saw twelve. Both accepted the vultures as heaven's sign, but Remus said the land was his—he had seen the birds first—while Romulus said he should have it because he had seen twice as many. The two fought. Romulus killed Remus but named Reims after him.

The myth is derived from a similar tale about the founding of Rome, to which Romulus is supposed to have given his own name. The legend of Sts. Sixte and Sinice is, however, close to the truth. It errs only in date and in ascribing to the saints a discipleship they never had. Sixte was a Roman missionary who, accompanied by Sinice, founded the first Christian community in Reims, in A.D. 260. On a hill near the Via Caesaria, Caesar's Way, which was the main road from Reims to Rome, Sixte built a small church over which he presided until his death in 280. Then his companion, Sinice, who had been installed in nearby Soissons, took over leadership of the Reims community.

Not until the beginning of the fourth century, however, when the Roman Emperor Constantine was converted to Christianity, did the religion begin to flourish and grow. Until then the Christians of Reims, ruled by Roman legions, were liable to persecution for their faith, as were all Christians in the Roman Empire. In the year 314, Betause, who was at that time the bishop of Reims's small band of Christians, took swift advantage of the new climate provided by Constantine's conversion. He moved the remote hilltop church to a prominent spot in the center of town, not far from the site of the present cathedral.

About one hundred years later, another bishop, Nicaise, had a basilica built in precisely the spot where today's cathedral stands. Excavations made while repairing the cathedral after extensive bomb damage in World War I uncovered the basilica's foundations. Their measurements showed that it occupied about half the space of the present structure and probably stood about half as high. Bishop Nicaise made this basilica his cathedral. On its doorstep, in the year 406, he died, a martyr. The city was surrounded by Vandal tribesmen, plundering their way from Germany to Spain. Through Gaul, as the Romans called France, lay the most direct route. The Roman Empire was disintegrating. All over, barbarians were taking possession of the pieces. Reims was one they hoped for.

Swinging axlike halberds, the Vandal warriors stormed the city gates. Gaining access, they pushed to the heart of the city, where they met Nicaise at the cathedral threshold. He was reciting the forty-fourth psalm from the Bible's Book of Psalms. "For our soul is bowed down to the dust: our belly cleaveth unto the earth." As he said the words, one of the Vandals sliced off his head. Legend insists that as his severed head rolled on the cobblestones, the mouth audibly continued with the next verse of the psalm: "Arise for our help, and redeem us for thy mercies' sake."

The Bishop's sister, Eutropie, and several of the cathedral staff stood nearby. It is said that Eutropie threw herself on her brother's assassin, clawed out his eyes with her finger-nails, and flung them to the pavement, where they rolled in the Bishop's blood. One of the invaders slashed her throat, whereupon the cathedral staff turned on him and those near him and tore out their eyes. The superstitious tribesmen feared some supernatural vengeance had descended upon them. In terror, they fled the town.

Reims was saved from a ruthless sacking, and Nicaise and Eutropie were sainted. The stone on which Nicaise's head had come to rest was moved from the street to a position of honor in the cathedral floor in front of the altar. Statues of the Bishop and his sister stand just to the left of a central statue of St. Sixte at the main door of the cathedral's north entrance. Nicaise holds his severed head in his hands, the eyes looking up to the benign smile of an accompanying angel.

Directly opposite the statues of Nicaise and Eutropie stands another angel-guarded figure: St. Remi. Statues of this saint ornament many of France's cathedrals, and panes in stained-glass windows retell the story of his life—with good reason, for he baptized the first King of the French, helping to found the nation and making its ruler the supreme authority under God. To Reims, however, where he was born, lived to a ripe old age, and died, he belongs first of all.

Tales of the miraculous surround his name from even before his birth. Supposedly his parents, like the parents of John the Baptist, who announced the coming of Christ, were too old to bear children. But a hermit visited Remi's mother, Cilinie, and told her he had been informed in a dream by no less a person than Christ Himself that she was to become the mother of a saint. This story was recorded, although not until some five hundred years later, by a scholar educated in the cathedral school at Reims who subsequently became a monk. The monk, Flodoard, was put in charge of the cathedral archives. From a helter-skelter mass of material, he composed a history of Christianity in Reims, beginning with the days of Sixte and Sinice. His work includes a particularly large section on the life and accomplishments of St. Remi.

Flodoard tells us that Remi became Bishop of Reims at the age of twenty-two, despite the saint's own protests that he was much too young for the office. "He was," Flodoard wrote, "less elected than carried to his post. He was carried to the cathedral on the shoulders of his fellow townspeople, there to be ordained." Flodoard pictures Remi as a handsome young man "with a countenance full of joy."

This handsome youth becomes very much alive in the monk's text, his personality crashing through the confinement of the cramped Latin characters in which manuscripts of the day were inscribed. He had, it seems, always the courage of his convictions and was ever prompt to reproach those whom he considered wrongdoers—but so gently that he attracted rather than alienated them. He took much pleasure in the natural world around him. In the fifth century A.D. he was preaching the doctrine of conservation. This beautiful world, he said, was a gift of God which man had the responsibility to preserve. He upbraided farmers who overworked their fields; he abhorred the hunting of wild animals. He taught sparrows to eat from his hand.

Remi is credited with the first of his miracles shortly after being ordained bishop. He was attending the wedding party of a cousin when a servant came to him, bemoaning that the wine had run out. He asked to be taken to the wine cellar. There he knelt by an empty barrel, made the sign of the cross on it, and prayed. When he turned the tap, wine gushed out. The saint's grateful cousin willed extensive land to the cathedral.

Many miracles of healing are attributed to Remi. One story tells of a sick man who came to him to be baptized. "Remi wished," wrote Flodoard, "to give the sick man health of both soul and body." After the baptism the saint looked for the oil used to anoint the sick while praying for their recovery. Finding all the oil vessels empty, he placed them on the altar and prayed. Slowly, the vessels filled. Remi anointed the sick man and cured him.

Another time he is said to have quenched a fire that threatened to destroy the entire city. When, despite desperate efforts to put out the flames, a third of Reims lay in ashes, a committee of citizens came to Remi for help. He prayed at the cathedral altar; then, hoisting a cross to his shoulder, he went to the scene of the blaze and walked into it. The flames receded before him. So says Flodoard.

Not all Remi's miracles were so charitable. There is a legend that this man of conviction once punished an entire township for disobeying his order to store wheat against a forthcoming famine he had been warned about in a dream. He subjected all the men of the township to hernias and all the women to goiters for four hundred years. On another occasion, when a miller objected to having part of the property he worked given by his lord to the Church, Remi is supposed to have made the man's mill wheel turn backward.

A good many of the miracles attributed to Remi have the ring of familiar Bible stories. Just as his conception in his mother's later years recalls the conception of John the Baptist, so the filling of the wine barrel at a wedding recalls a similar miracle performed by Christ at a wedding feast in Cana. The receding flames have something in common with the receding waters of the Red Sea, through which the Bible's Book of Exodus tells us the Israelites were able safely to escape from slavery in Egypt. The curse of goiters and hernias echoes another part of Exodus, in which boils are visited on the slavemasters of the Israelites. The dream warning of famine has overtones of the passage in the Book of Genesis in which a dream of an Egyptian ruler is interpreted by a captive Israelite, Joseph, as a prophecy of famine. The ruler puts Joseph in charge of storing crops and the famine is averted. Remi's biographers knew their Bible stories, though a Bible in print was yet centuries off.

Remi's great claim to fame, however, rests not on legends of miracles, however charming, but on the historical triumph of his conversion to Christianity of Clovis, King of the tribal French, the Franks. The Franks had fought their way to supremacy over the Gallic tribes who had divided Roman lands among themselves after the breakup of the empire. Under Clovis they began the job of forging the nation to which they gave their name.

Clovis pieced and glued into one state tribal territories equal to about half the present area of France. He pieced with ruthless might and glued with cunning strategy. Brilliant, despotic, he looked every inch his part. As head of his tribe he was entitled to a special hairdo: long locks which fell loose to his shoulders, then were braided to the waist. A symbol of his authority, this hair style was a carry-over from early pagan belief that long hair, in imitation of long solar rays, was pleasing to the sun god. The same belief applied to the ferocious Clovian mustache, which drooped to the top of his braids. His helmet was horned like a bull's head. His leather sandals were laced to the thighs, where they met his mini-length tunic. The blue cloak over his shoulders was draped back from a shield which he carried by slipping his left arm through three brackets on the shield's inner surface. His halberd and heavy sword were never far from his reach.

Historians disagree on the time and circumstances of this

powerful ruler's switch in allegiance from a pagan to a Christian god, but not about Remi's major role in it. Flodoard tells the story this way.

Clovis's wife, Clotilda, had long been trying to convert him to Christianity, but, judges Flodoard, "as a woman she lacked the strength to pierce the heart of a barbarian." Then a day came when the Frankish chieftain and his army were deadlocked in fierce battle with a Germanic tribe attempting to invade the kingdom Clovis had begun to establish. The chieftain begged his gods for victory—but victory did not come. As the battle stalemated through a long day, the courage of the Franks began to fail. Clovis's men fought more and more feebly. Their commander remembered his wife's pleas. Could her god turn the tide? He would see. He offered Christ a treaty of mutual allegiance: "Thou who art, according to Clotilda, the son of the living God, help me in my distress, and if thou givest me the victory I will believe in thee and be baptized in thy name."

No sooner had the statement left his lips than the tide of battle turned and the courage of his men revived. The leader of the German tribe was killed; his soldiers fled in disarray. Triumphant but humbled, Clovis returned to his wife, saying, "Clovis has conquered the Germans, but you have conquered Clovis." And Clotilda sent for St. Remi to prepare her husband for baptism, which was administered on Easter Eve.

Flodoard's story is as debatable as it is dramatic. It appears likely that Clovis's reason for embracing his wife's religion was far more ambitious than the winning of a single battle. By accepting Christianity he won support from a powerful group of bishops in his goal of protecting and even expanding his kingdom. By promising to extend the dominion of Christendom to pagans, he sanctified military conquest of their homelands.

But the coin of this bargain had another side. At the same time that Clovis made friends with bishops, he had to be careful not to make enemies among the pagans in his own land, particularly among his troops. The true story seems to be that he invited St. Remi to prepare him for baptism in secret. Meanwhile, he persuaded his pagan soldiers that Christianity could strengthen their skills in battle. Ultimately, three thousand of his troops were baptized with him. The event took place not at Easter time, as Flodoard had it, but on Christmas Eve in the year 496. We are certain of the date because it is mentioned in correspondence between Clovis and a bishop for whose help he was especially eager, since this bishop was in charge of congregations in an area Clovis considered weak: the valley of the Vienne River, on the chieftain's southwest flank.

The baptism was spectacular, attended by all the bishops Clovis was wooing. The night before the ceremony, he, his Queen, and several of their household went to a chapel in the cathedral to pray with Remi. Flodoard throws a mystic as well as a nationalistic aura around the praying. He says that as the group knelt, light filled the chapel and a voice was heard saying, "Peace be with you. Fear nothing. Remain in my love." The King and Queen threw themselves on the floor, trembling. The light faded except for an afterglow on the face of Remi, who prophesied that Clovis's conquests would become the foundation for a nation, as indeed they did.

The next day the route from the palace to the cathedral was canopied with veils, carpeted with velvet, and hung with tapestries. Priests carrying crosses and bishops with their crooks held aloft led the procession, chanting hymns. Then came Remi and Clovis, hand in hand. They were followed by the Queen, the couple's son Theodoric, and Clovis's sisters, Alboflède and Landehile. The latter three were also to be baptized. Bringing up the rear marched the three thousand soldiers.

The procession and the onlookers so crowded the streets that the bearer of the oil with which Clovis was to be anointed was unable to press his way through to the cathedral. But Remi was at no loss as to what to do. He prayed. Whereupon, legend insists—and it is a legend that was venerated for fourteen centuries in France—a dove flew down from the cathedral rafters with a vial of oil in its beak. So pervasive was the perfume of that oil that it scented the entire cathedral. Succeeding generations considered it to be holy. It was preserved and drops of it used in the consecration ceremonies of the thirty-five royal rulers of France who were crowned at Reims. Only sixteen were crowned elsewhere.

Sculptors of later ages displayed their vision of the baptism of Clovis high on the cathedral's main façade, front center in the Gallery of Kings. This gallery is a line of six-ton, fifteen-foot-high statues which extends around three sides. Clovis, nude, stands in a tublike baptismal font. At his left, Clotilda offers him the crown of France. At his right, St. Remi smiles. Arrayed farther to right and left are the toga-clad figures of the monarchs who succeeded Clovis up until the early thirteenth century, when the figures were carved. The baptismal scene is repeated on a smaller scale above the north portal of the cathedral and on sixteenth-century tapestries inside. Also, at the north entrance, above the center door, are carvings of seven more of Remi's spiritual triumphs, miracles of healing and the filling of the wine barrel among them.

The otherworldliness of this evangelist who converted the ruler of the Frankish kingdom did not, however, interfere with his amassing considerable holdings in this world. In fact, the foot in heaven seems automatically to have enriched the foot on earth. Of the fifteen villages of which he was lord, two were given him by Clovis. Remi's will mentions them as "tokens of the King's affection." Another, the will says, was bought for five thousand pounds of silver. Other properties listed included forests, fields, and pastureland in the Vosges Mountains, some 175 miles southeast of Reims. The will remarks chattily that the Bishop was "fortunate in obtaining these through the graceful offices of several skillful go-betweens."

All this property Remi left to the cathedral, his "dear and holy inheritor." Throughout the document, he addresses the cathedral as a person, using a form of address usually reserved for the family, for children, or for close friends. To Remi the cathedral was all three.

Witnessed by nine clergy and seven laymen, the long will—the third Remi had written, keeping pace with his growing estate—is finely detailed. It gives freedom to fourteen of his twenty-four slaves, slavery being a Roman custom which the Gauls had not yet outgrown. His remaining ten slaves are left half and half to his nephews and his dear and holy inheritor. To it also he leaves the laborers bound to his service, workers who were one step up from slavery. Remi's laborers included the men Dagarède, Profuturus, Prudence, Provinçiole, Temnaic, Maurilion, Baudoleif, and the women Naviatène, Lauta, Suffronia. All but one of these names are either Latin, the language of the Romans, or Gallic, which was the basis of French. But the name of the exception, Baudoleif, marks him as a Norseman who perhaps had been captured in a raid on the coast of France.

The Bishop left much more treasure to his cathedral: all his fine table linen, his silver spoons, and his extensive vineyards. He was ninety-six when he died, a more than remarkable age in a time when widespread disease, ignorance of hygiene, wars, and daily brutality made death a commonplace and forty a ripe old age. His long life was historically important not only to France but to all Europe. By uniting throne and Church, Remi cleared the way for what was to become, some three centuries later, the Holy Roman Empire. That empire was founded by King Charlemagne of France, who, with the slogan "Christianity or Death," annexed for his country pagan territory that included what is

now Switzerland and about half of modern Germany and
Italy.

On Christmas Day, in the year 800, Pope Leo III blessed
Charlemagne's conquests as a means of spreading the doctrine of Christ. Placing a crown on the King's head, he pronounced him no longer merely King of France but "the
great and pacific Emperor of the Romans, crowned by God."
Thereafter, for more than eight hundred years, the monarchs of Europe vied with each other in bloody battle and
wily politics to win this title and the power and wealth which
it could help them accumulate.

Within France the forty-six-year-long reign of Charlemagne restored to Reims, as to all religious institutions, a
dignity that had been lost after the death of Clovis. Lacking
that monarch's strong and practiced hand, the Frankish
kingdom had fallen apart in fierce tribal war. Bishops of
Reims sided now with this chieftain, now with that one. Some
bishops were also military commanders. One, Egidius, acted
as a roving ambassador for the tribal king Childebert, and was
dismissed for making exaggerated claims for expenses. The
behavior of the clergy was so unclerical that when Tilpin,
the man who served as archbishop* for most of Charlemagne's reign, came to office, he had to issue a decree for-
bidding the cathedral staff to "frequent taverns of ill repute
and wander about like tramps."

Tilpin and Charlemagne were good friends. The Em-

---

* Reims became an archbishopric in 749.

peror admired the Archbishop's learning, and the Archbishop admired the Emperor's encouragement of learning. Charlemagne established schools throughout the land, at one of which, held in his own palace, he himself learned to read and write. Another he founded in Reims, under the wing of the cathedral. This was the school where Flodoard and a long line of scholars received their education. The cathedral school of Reims was among the best—and certainly the most democratic—in medieval Europe.

The philosophy of the school was first laid down in a long letter to Tilpin which Charlemagne dictated. He asked that only those teachers be hired who would make of their profession "a science combining the desire to instruct with the knowledge of how to do it." He insisted that the school be open to all the children of the community, including those of peasant farmers, or serfs, the lowest class of medieval society. This was a radical insistence. Formerly, such education as was available had been strictly limited to children of the nobility and candidates for the clergy.

Arguing against the popular notion of his time that it was better for the masses to work with their hands than with their heads, Charlemagne said in his letter to Tilpin: "While it is of course better to do than merely to know, it is necessary to know before one can do." Tilpin readily agreed. To help achieve the Emperor's objectives, he made an important change in the writing normally used to copy manuscripts. At the Reims school the difficult-to-decipher, crowded, angular script of previous ages was loosened up and rounded over. People were able to learn to read more easily when letters were spaced out, sentences uncramped.

At Christmas time, four years after Charlemagne had been crowned Emperor in Rome, Tilpin arranged for an anniversary celebration of the event at Reims. Mindful of the Reims tradition as the sanctifier of monarchs, which Remi had established, he persuaded Pope Leo III to journey north from Rome, braving the treacherous snows of the Alps, to help him conduct a special Mass.

The ceremony was imposing. Charlemagne, the principal figure, normally scorned the wearing of gold and jewels, but on this occasion he gave in to Tilpin's urging that he should wear them to honor not himself but his God. As he knelt before the altar, his wide, multi-gemmed armbands gleamed in the candlelight. A flowing blue cape billowed from his shoulders and spread out in an arc on the floor behind him. It was fastened with a ruby-studded gold clasp; the scabbard of his sword glittered with sapphires. Underneath the blue cape he wore scarlet breeches and a vest of otter skins over a white tunic. As the Pope bent to make the sign of the cross on the forehead of the Emperor-King, the congregation cried, "Long live our King and Emperor." Crowds in the square outside echoed the cry in successive waves of sound that rolled through the still air of the winter-bound town.

Perhaps it was the majesty of this scene, coupled with his admiration for Charlemagne's ability and principles, that inspired Tilpin to begin writing a saga of the King's accomplishments. Three centuries later popular court storytellers of France drew on this saga to fashion the rhymed tale of

the *Gestes du Roi Charlemagne,* the Deeds of King Charlemagne. In the most famous part of this tale, the *Song of
Roland,* Tilpin himself still lives, his name changed slightly
to Archbishop Turpin.

The *Song of Roland* opens in Charlemagne's court in the
south of France. Messengers arrive from Marsile, a Moorish king of Spain. The Moors, originally from Northern
Africa, were, in Charlemagne's time, in possession of a large
part of Spain. Charlemagne planned to conquer them and
convert them from their Moslem religion to Christianity. In
the *Song of Roland* Marsile's messengers bring an offer of
surrender to Charlemagne's court. Charlemagne calls a
council of his nobles to discuss the offer. His nephew, Roland, argues against accepting. He scents deception. But
another baron, Ganelon, persuades the King that the offer
is legitimate. Having lost the debate to Ganelon, Roland
feels honor-bound to volunteer to deliver the acceptance.
He, Archbishop Turpin, and a close companion, Olivier,
set out for Spain with 20,000 *"Français de France,"*
the flower of the younger generation of the Frankish kingdom. Meanwhile, Ganelon, who is in truth a traitor in the
pay of Marsile, sends the Moorish King secret word, in-
forming him where the youthful band can be trapped.

In a high pass in the Pyrenees Mountains, which divide
France from Spain, Marsile and 100,000 soldiers set upon
the 20,000 Franks. Olivier urges Roland to blow his horn, an
alarm previously arranged with Charlemagne to signal the
need for reinforcements, but Roland is too proud to admit

that help is necessary. In battle, he slices off the right hand of Marsile, who flees. Then Roland slays Marsile's son and heir. In three successive encounters, the Franks rout the Moors, but at the price of their own lives. A fatally wounded Roland gathers up his dead to be blessed by the dying Archbishop. Then, finally and feebly, Roland blows his horn, in the hope that Charlemagne will hear and come to see the results of Ganelon's treachery. He lifts his right hand to God, and the archangel Gabriel descends to bear his soul to Paradise.

The incident which Tilpin and later writers magnified into this episode was Charlemagne's march on Spain in 778. Receiving word in the midst of the march that his kingdom at home was endangered by attacking Saxon tribes, Charlemagne retreated. During the retreat the Moors set upon his rear guard, which was commanded by his nephew, Roland, and slaughtered it.

The storytellers' embellishment of this bit of history reflects a code which ruled the Middle Ages, not only in France but in all Europe. The code was born in Reims when Remi baptized Clovis, uniting throne and Rome. It was formalized when Charlemagne became Holy Roman Emperor. The code was: loyalty to God and King is one and the same thing. Kings were kings "by the Grace of God"—a phrase coined by Charlemagne—and they and the Popes shared, or sometimes tussled over, the honor of representing Him on earth. It followed that to be the Roland type of daredevil-at-arms in behalf of one's king was to be pure of soul.

The *Song of Roland* and the saga of which the song is the gem started a pattern for similar tales. Other clergy followed Tilpin's example of idealizing in verse the "soldier of God" with a divine mission to defend and expand Christendom, i.e., the Holy Roman Empire. Later, the recitation of these tales became after-dinner diversion in the courts of nobles, but at first they were read mainly in churches and military encampments. Both Church and monarch had much to gain by inspiring soldiers. Monarchs wanted land. The Church, which had no army, could, by using the army of a Christian king, expand its influence at no cost. The monarch, in turn, could have his acquisitiveness blessed by the Church. So long did this custom continue that as much later as 1066 the French Norman, William the Conqueror, took care to have the *Song of Roland* recited to his troops before leading them, with a bishop at his side, into the Battle of Hastings. There he defeated the King of England and usurped his crown. The takeover was supported by Pope Alexander, to whose authority William had promised to return rebellious English clergy.

Still later, a similar alliance promoted the Crusades of the twelfth and thirteenth centuries. Their announced purpose was to capture from the Moslems and hand over to Christendom the holy city of Jerusalem, and no doubt there were some who were inspired by this zeal. But for many, a Crusade was an effort to shift control of Mediterranean shipping from Moslem to European merchants—plus an opportunity to loot stores of Moslem riches.

As long as this mutually profitable understanding be-

tween medieval Church and state lasted, archbishops of
Reims continued to be powerful links in the chain. Their
position called for a headquarters worthy of their power, a
requirement which by the beginning of the ninth century
posed a problem. The basilica which Nicaise had conceived
four centuries earlier was showing the cracks and concavities
of age. Besides, architectural styles were beginning to change.
If Reims was to maintain its lead, there was work to be
done. Fortunately, there was also, in the year 820, the man
to do it.

II

The Cathedral Grows

Ebban, Archbishop of Reims in the year 820, was thought to be the illegitimate son of Charlemagne's son and heir, Louis. Ebban was a prelate bent on maintaining Reims's distinction, but much troubled by the cost of doing so. He had a budget problem, for despite Reims's lofty position, it was not rich. Thousands of tons of stone were needed for the necessary repair work. The nearest quarry was some thirty miles distant, set in an arc of hills across the river Marne. Oxcarts were the means of transport. The largest of the carts could carry no more than one and one third tons of rock, and the fastest team of yoked oxen could travel no more than nine miles a day. A speedier alternative was river transport, but tolls charged by landowners along the riverbanks upped the cost of this method by three percent. Ebban couldn't afford the surcharge, so he decided to rely on the oxcarts—but to rally them by the hundreds.

He persuaded whole congregations to volunteer their help. Often a procession from quarry to cathedral would be made up of five or six congregations, each with a priest in charge. Tales of miraculous happenings en route began to spread through the countryside. One group claimed that the Virgin Mary lighted torches for them in the sky at night. Another reported that St. Remi had calmed a storm that threatened their progress. Parishioners from the village of Bergères-les-Vertus insisted that the springtime flood-waters of the Marne had been made to recede to let them cross.

As each procession arrived in Reims, Ebban held a special Mass, granting forgiveness of sins to all participants. News of this development spread as rapidly as the growing accounts of the miraculous. The parades of carts multiplied. At first Ebban was overjoyed. Twelve months later he was disillusioned. No matter how many eager volunteers, they never seemed able to keep up with the need for supply. The loads they could carry, the speeds at which they could travel were simply too limited. Stonemasons idled, waiting for material. Furthermore, the volunteers were amateurs who didn't know one grade of rock from another. They frequently brought such poor grades that the rock was useless. At this rate Ebban would never see the job completed.

He was a discouraged man when, quite literally, he stumbled on a solution for the dilemma. One morning he mounted the towering, four-foot-thick ramparts of the wall which the Romans had built around Reims. He tripped; his foot dislodged a stone. He picked it up, marveling. There, right there, was his stone supply. Promptly he applied to King Louis, his presumed father, for permission to tear down the wall. Permission was granted. The old wall supplied even more stone than was needed, and Ebban began to dream of additions to the cathedral. The King gave him permission to shut off neighboring streets, thus making room for a cloister and clergy residences. He lent the Archbishop a court architect, one Rumaud, to design the layout and supervise construction.

Rumaud quickly saw a lifetime opportunity. He suggested to Ebban that the repair work then in progress was mere patchwork. Really, he said, the cathedral should be reconstructed from the ground up. Ebban accepted the suggestion. He recruited laborers from every corner of the kingdom, gave them free lodging, and persuaded townspeople to keep them provided with food and wine. From King Louis he secured a decree stating that certain taxes from Reims, which normally went into the royal treasury, were to be paid instead to the cathedral. These financed the work.

In gratitude, Ebban arranged for Pope Stephen to consecrate Louis as Holy Roman Emperor at Reims. Pope and King met outside the cathedral, dismounting from their horses. Louis threw himself flat on the ground three times. The third time Pope Stephen raised him to his feet and the two men embraced. Then they entered the cathedral. The Pope prayed long for the well-being of the monarch, after which he anointed Louis with the oil used at the baptism of Clovis and placed on his head a jeweled crown which he had brought as a present. Louis's Queen, Hermingarde, he also crowned with a golden circlet, his gift to her. Having completed the coronation, the Pope, accompanied by the choir, chanted in Latin: *"Laudamus; volumus; fiat,"* that is to say, we approve; we wish it; let it be done. The congregation responded in French, *"Nous approuvons; nous voulons que cela soit."* We approve; we want it to be.

Ebban ordered Rumaud to immortalize this coronation scene in mosaic on the front façade of the cathedral. However, the Archbishop never saw the final fruits of his endeavors. In 835 he was deposed, having supported the wrong candidate during a dispute in the royal family over which of Louis's three legitimate sons should succeed to the throne. Six years later Ebban returned to Reims, briefly, when the son to whom he had tied his fortunes won, briefly, an upper hand. However, he was soon ousted again and ended his days in the far west of the kingdom as court chaplain for one of his half brothers.

For four years thereafter the cathedral was watched over by only a priest and a clerk, but at the end of that time a man capable of continuing Ebban's work became archbishop. He was Hincmar, a young monk from the Abbey of Saint-Denis, near Paris. The influence of King Charles the Bald elevated him to office. This Charles, the son of Louis by a second marriage, had been catapulted to the throne by a mother who combined sex appeal with political know-how. She persuaded her adoring husband that the best way to end the feud among the three sons by his former marriage over the question of succession was to name as heir the son of his new marriage, Charles.

Hincmar had long been the Prince's friend. He rose with him. A man of tremendous drive, he set out to make the Archbishop of Reims the most influential personage in France after the King, and the city of Reims the spiritual capital of the country. As described by Benedictine monks in the nearby Abbey of Saint-Maur, Hincmar was a complicated personality. In a document recording cathedral history of the day, the monks commented: "One sees in Hincmar a lively spirit, subtle, keen, broad, capable of great achievements; a man of superior understanding and of disciplined living. These qualities, combined with the eminence of his dignity, make him shine among all other prelates of his time and have attracted to him the respect of Popes and Kings. But one also discovers in him an inflexible character, crafty and capable of deceit, utterly dedicated to the attainment of his own ends and brooking no opposition. His cunning politics maneuver everything to the advancement of his aims and designs." Not only cunning, Hincmar could, if provoked, be ruthless. He demanded unquestioning and absolute allegiance from his clergy, and when his own nephew, the Bishop of Laon, refused to obey him, he had him imprisoned and blinded.

Hincmar inherited from Ebban a cathedral solid in structure but sparse in adornment. To amass beautification funds, he called into play all his wealthy connections—far more impressive a list than any of which his predecessors could boast. Able to spend with a free hand, he covered the roof in *plomb,* a lead compound, over which he laid marble tiling. He made the windows glow with stained glass and warmed the ceiling with rich paintings. He procured a golden altar cloth, sewn with emeralds and rubies. The altar cross he had cast in solid gold, inset with diamonds and sapphires. Other crosses, carried in processions by clergy and acolytes, were of silver, also glittering with jewels. Vases on the altar gleamed in both gold and silver, gem-encrusted. The manuscripts from which the Bible was read were decorated with gold and ivory.

In 862, Hincmar's handiwork was complete. At a command celebration of the Mass, attended by all the clergy of the area and by King Charles the Bald, Hincmar dedicated the renovated cathedral. We are again indebted to the monks of Saint-Maur for pungent comments on the occasion: "The glory of the Archbishop in regal robes outshone that of the monarch. His attire and his bearing suggested to the assembled people the Glory to whom this work of art was being dedicated." This was Hincmar's day.

The two archbishops who followed Hincmar further enlavished his triumphs. The first, Foulques, doubled as chancellor and minister to King Charles the Simple and thus had easy access to royal generosity. His first act as archbishop was to enlarge the cathedral school started by Tilpin under Charlemagne. To the cathedral proper he added more paintings and more stained glass. Then he turned his attention to the city wall Ebban had torn down. This he rebuilt completely.

Foulques had good reason to feel the need of a protecting wall. Europe was a caldron boiling with feuds. The German and French sections of the Holy Roman Empire were threatening each other. The Italian section, encouraged by this row between more powerful neighbors, was watching for a chance to grab the imperial crown. The French monarch was at the mercy of his nobles, some of whom had enough power to set up rival kings if they so chose.

Among the most powerful of these nobles was Baldwin, Count of Flanders. Though part of the Kingdom of France, Flanders, under Baldwin, sympathized with the Germans, who refused to recognize Charles the Simple either as King of France or as Emperor. In retaliation, Charles seized from Baldwin the Abbey of Saint-Wast, coveted for its productive vineyards, and turned it over to his archbishop. Whereupon Baldwin hired an assassin who, stalking Foulques as he returned from his daily conference with the King, set upon him and stabbed him to death.

Foulques's successor, Archbishop Herivée, is extolled by the historian Flodoard as "combining magnetism of appearance with magnetism of soul." Flodoard calls Herivée "a father of the clergy, protector of all people and the courageous defender of the flock entrusted to him." A young man, evidently with a great deal of charisma, the new Archbishop also possessed an enviable voice that made his chanting of psalms a great attraction in the cathedral. He had excellent taste and brought the Hincmar décor to the height of perfection. More jewels were added to the cross, and an altar of pure silver was built in the center of the choir space. Gold and silver candelabra were suspended from the rafters. The bare walls were softened with silken hangings. The collection of gem-studded vases was vastly enlarged.

Not only was Herivée a man of taste, he was also an excellent administrator. He saw to it that the granaries and wine cellars of the cathedral community were kept well stocked, that villages which belonged to the cathedral were kept in good repair. "He governed all church property with wisdom," wrote Flodoard.

To the cathedral of Reims and its diocese, the territory subject to it, people looked as toward an island of prestige and prosperity in a kingdom rent by rivalries. However shaky and jealous the opposing states, they did have one linking heritage: belief in the union of God and monarch—and Reims was the guardian of this heritage. The cathedral protected it through war, murder, fire, and foul play until the French Revolution in 1789. The ceremonies that visibly symbolized this invisible heritage were, of course, the consecrations with the oil of Remi.

In troublesome times it became more important than ever that these ceremonies be carried out with memorable splendor. It was also important that the splendor become traditional. And so in 1059, the then Archbishop of Reims, Gervais, wrote what was, in effect, a scenario for the consecration of kings at Reims. Not until 121 years later did the scenario receive official approval in the form of a royal decree that this was *the* consecration format and Reims was *the* cathedral in which it was to be followed. Nevertheless, by custom, interim monarchs accepted the Gervais formula and Reims's exclusive right to sanctify the crown.

When the ceremony as conceived by Gervais is about to begin, the kingdom's nobles enter the cathedral. Coronets glitter on their heads. Their violet velvet mantles, ermine-trimmed and satin-lined, trail behind them as they march down the aisles. Their costumes have been precisely prescribed. Following these lords come the Queen and her ladies-in-waiting. They are seated in the sanctuary to the right of the altar. The left side is occupied by the Archbishop, bishops, and representatives of the Pope. In the center sit monks of the Abbey of Saint-Rémy.

While these groups are finding seats, the cathedral canons, who are its legal counselors, plus two bishops accompanied by two choirboys, fetch the King from the adjacent palace of the Archbishop. One choirboy knocks once loudly on the door of the King's chambers. The King's Chamberlain, his personal servant, replies, "What do you require?" The Bishop of Laon answers, "The King." The second choirboy knocks. Twice. The three knocks of the two boys, said Gervais in a rubric, or marginal note in his script, "represent the three persons of the Christian Trinity: God, the Father and Creator; Christ, His Son; and the Holy Spirit, or the action of Father and Son in this world."

When the King arrives, the Archbishop begins a sermon on the demands of the Christian faith. At the end, he turns to the King and asks if he is prepared to accept these demands. When the King agrees, the Archbishop reads aloud an oath of allegiance to the Church and to the subjects of the land. This he hands to the King to sign on the altar. The oath, inscribed on parchment and bound in silver filigreed with gold, reads:

I, by the Grace of God, King of the French, on this day of my Consecration, promise before God and His Saints

that I will protect for each of you his rights and
privileges, and that I will, with God's aid, defend you,
as every King who has at heart the welfare of the
Church and its Bishops should do in his Kingdom.
I promise further to render to the people who are
entrusted to my care true justice according to law
and custom.

The Archbishop next reminds the assemblage of Reim's exclusive right to consecrate the kings of France. He lifts from the altar the sword of Charlemagne, the scabbard sheathed in white velvet embroidered with the royal symbol of France—the fleur-de-lis. Removing the sheath, he hands the golden-hilted sword in its gold scabbard to the country's High Marshal, the highest legal authority in the land. The Marshal draws the sword and holds it point upward for the rest of the ceremony. Now comes the consecration's most sacred moment. The vial of oil, safeguarded between coronations by the monks of the Abbey of Saint-Rémy, is presented to the Archbishop by the Abbot. He offers it on a white cushion draped with a cloth of silver brocade. Using a gold needle, the Archbishop extracts a few drops of oil from the vial and mixes these with ordinary oil, which has been blessed at the altar. With the mixture he anoints the monarch. First, he touches the King's head, praying "that His Majesty should be endowed with wisdom"; then his breast, "that His Majesty may share the love of God"; then each shoulder, "that His Majesty may willingly bear burdens for his people"; his elbows, "that His Majesty may fight for God"; and the palms of his hands, "that His Majesty may labor well for his God." The intertwining of royal responsibilities toward heaven and earth in this blessing was no accident. Gervais's intent was to solidify for the future the heritage of Reims's past.

Having completed the Church's consecration, the Gervais script gives the King's subjects their turn. Do they accept this man as their monarch? The question is put individually to the nobles and clergy of the realm, and each gives his individual reply. The questioning starts with the noblest of the nobles and the highest ranking of the clergy, then descends the scale. When the last yes has been heard—there is no record of any no—the cathedral doors are thrown wide open. As many as possible of the masses outside press in. Do they, too, accept this king? The question is posed and they respond in a roaring chorus.

With the agreement of the kingdom, then, the King is crowned. Over his shoulders is draped a mantle embroidered with fleurs-de-lis, containing portions of Charlemagne's mantle. It is clasped by a gold pin, set with eighteen rubies, eighteen diamonds, and eighteen pearls. Charlemagne's crown, red-velvet-lined, is set upon the monarch's head. Sapphire-encrusted, the front of the crown peaks into a gold fleur-de-lis, lustered with thirty-six pearls. Charlemagne's gold scepter, ivory-handled and glowing with rubies and pearls, is placed in the King's right hand.

As the crown is set upon His Majesty's head, trumpets

sound. A flock of birds is let loose from the cathedral rafters in commemoration of St. Remi's dove. Pages move through the crowd distributing gold and silver medallions.

In later centuries, the firing of cannons at the moment of coronation was added to the Gervais script. But otherwise the ceremony remained much the same. It was always followed by a feast in the Archbishop's palace. The next day the new King went about laying his hands on the sick, for the belief was that kings, having been crowned by the Grace of God, had the power of healing in their fingertips.

Revered as Reims was, thanks in great part to the mysticism of the coronation ritual, the cathedral could not entirely escape the consequences of violence in the kingdom at large. Indeed, ever since Nicaise's head had rolled in the cathedral square, bloodshed seemed a part of its inheritance. No one was overly astounded when, in 1192, Reims became the scene of a pomp-filled funeral for a young cathedral clergyman, treacherously murdered.

He was Albert of Louvain, archdeacon of the church of St. Lambert, in the town of Liége. He had been elected bishop by the town clergy over the opposition of a minority. The Holy Roman Emperor of the day, a German, Henry VI, saw a chance to extend his influence westward by siding with the opposing minority. He named a German priest for the post. Albert appealed to the Pope, who gave him letters to the Archbishops of Cologne and Reims. The letter to the Archbishop of Cologne commanded that prelate to consecrate Albert. The letter to the Archbishop of Reims was for emergency use, in case—as the Pope quite rightly suspected—the Archbishop of Cologne should be too afraid of the Emperor to carry out the Pope's orders.

On the other hand—as the Pope also suspected—the Archbishop of Reims, William of Champagne, was delighted with the chance to defy the Emperor. He ordained Albert with the widest publicity he could muster. "The ordination took place," wrote a local historian, "in the presence of all the nobility thereabouts." The new Bishop was given refuge at Reims and a position on the cathedral staff.

All was going well for the young man. Nevertheless, William warned him, the Emperor's pride had been wounded and he would almost certainly seek revenge. Albert should be careful where he went and what he did. He should not trust strangers.

But Albert was the trusting type. He was gentle-natured, friendly, and outgoing. He made friends with three Germans who arrived in Reims, saying they were fleeing from the Emperor. One day he invited them to accompany him on the horseback ride which he was accustomed to take in the early mornings. Partway into the countryside, they turned on him and hacked him to death with their swords. Two French companions who had been late in joining the group caught up just as the assassins were fleeing. The French gave chase, but in vain. The Germans' horses were too fleet. The men made for Germany, where they delivered Albert's horse to the Emperor and received their pay.

In the sacristy of the cathedral, where clergy don their

robes, Albert's body was washed and clothed in white. After
an elaborate funeral he was buried under the cathedral floor
in front of the altar, beneath the stone on which Nicaise's
head had rolled.

The floor above his grave was an elaborate mosaic of intertwining leaves, branches, geometric figures, and scrolls, in
shades of yellow and henna. By the time of Albert's death,
the cathedral had been remodeled and redecorated beyond
even the most sumptuous dreams of Ebban and Hincmar.
The altar was set in a palatial chancel lighted by a seven-
branched chandelier suspended from a ring of crowns. The
chancel in turn adjoined a vaulted apse, decorated with
paintings, mosaics, and tremendous stained-glass windows.
Twenty of the windows were solemn portraits of kings of
France, each one accompanied by the archbishop who had
consecrated him. Garbed in ecclesiastical robes, the kings
could have been mistaken for priests, save for the swords
belted to their waists. The priestly resemblance was no hap-
penstance. It was intended to reinforce the concept of the
French monarchy's direct line to heaven, established by
Remi. At coronation time, these stern figures looked down
on the newest addition to their ranks as if in combined welcome and admonition.

To accommodate these various changes, the cathedral had,
by the end of the twelfth century, been considerably enlarged. Two great bays extended the nave. There was a
new main portal, and above it a new rose window gleamed

violet, blue, and ruby red. Outside the portal two new towers rose. On the façade below, statues carried out Reims's royal theme. Biblical kings, Solomon and David, were depicted kneeling for consecration and then rising to perform acts that were the will of God. High above these scenes, God, enthroned, bestowed on them His blessing.

Two archbishops, Adalberon and Samson, were responsible for these additions, by which the cathedral's squatness of earlier centuries was transformed into airy, soaring beauty. Samson, in particular, was a man of bold ideas. He was a close friend to Abbé Suger, the pioneering Abbot of Saint-Denis. Under Suger's direction, the first Gothic church in history was completed at Saint-Denis in 1144. Samson had been privileged to attend the dedication of that church. We know from some notes he kept that he had been deeply impressed by the triumphal procession of choirs and bishops which King Louis VII had led from the old abbey crypt to Suger's new wonder. He remembered the gasps of awe which the architecture drew from the throng—as well it might have. Instead of the fat columns supporting low ceilings to which worshippers were accustomed, slender pillars reached to a vaulted roof that seemed heaven-high. Instead of dungeon-thick walls with slits for windows, lacy fretwork, still powdered with stonecutters' dust, glowed with sunbeams refracted through stained glass. Outside, flying buttresses, arching from roof to ground, though strong as the bridges they resembled, were as graceful as butterflies' wings. They replaced the support once given by fortress-type walls and columns. Pointed spires, arrowing skyward, supplanted squared-off towers. This was the new, the modern style, the Gothic.

The dedication of Saint-Denis was not Samson's only exposure to the style. He had been head of the Cathedral Council at Chartres, just north of Paris, when that cathedral became Gothic. He wanted at Reims a Gothic cathedral that would outshine these and all the others now being built or rebuilt across the land.

Samson set to work like one possessed, but he finished only the towers and the great bays in the nave. His ambitions for the cathedral were not to be fulfilled in his lifetime. On May 6, in the year 1210, disaster struck. Fire! The cathedral of Samson, of Adalberon, Hincmar, and Ebban burned to the ground.

Much of the city burned with it. The Remois, though dismayed, were not discouraged. They had no intention of losing their standing as guardian of the French throne. There must be a new cathedral. Precisely a year later, on May 6, 1211, a new Archbishop (Samson had died) laid the cornerstone for the great Gothic cathedral that was to become the glory of all France.

The Archbishop, Aubri of Humbert, stood in pale sunlight, his vestments fluttering in a wind that had not yet lost winter's chill. He took a heavy building block from a man at his side. Stooping, he laid it in the still-blackened soil. A long shout went up from the crowds around him.

The man who handed over the building block was Jean

d'Orbais, the architect who conceived the design for the new Reims. Basically, his design was followed by all the architects who succeeded him in the next two centuries. While each new man brought his special talents to the task, none altered in any important respect the d'Orbais layout.

A year of frantic work had preceded the triumphal laying of the cornerstone. When the Archbishop had first called on the architect, Jean d'Orbais, observing the stricken town, had questioned where the money would come from. The Archbishop had replied, "From all France, with the aid of God." The architect sat down to his drawing board. Aubri of Humbert, meanwhile, had already sent letters near and far, requesting aid. In pulpits as distant as that of the cathedral of Saint-André in Bordeaux, almost 450 miles southwest of Reims, sermons were being preached asking congregations to contribute. The contributions were not always in cash. Salable jewels or rentable land were also welcome.

Nor was money the only necessity. The building of a Gothic cathedral also required mobilization of manpower and materials. In churches close by Reims, people were asked to donate labor and stone. The process was reciprocal. Parishes which came to the aid of Reims expected Reims to respond in kind, come their day of need. As one cathedral after another pointed spires to heaven, a network of mutual aid webbed across the country. It gave those who participated a sense of proprietorship, not just in local cathedrals but in all cathedrals.

This sense persists. Even though a modern archbishop of Reims may have to compete with the automobile for the attention of his own parishioners, scores of others across the country think of Reims as *their* national possession—as indeed it is, under Fine Arts supervision. The same feeling holds for the seventy-nine other Gothic marvels with which France set the style of cathedral building in the twelfth to fourteenth centuries. Though the echoes of history are louder in Reims than in any of the others, the French have no doubt that they own all eighty. These monuments to God are also monuments to the time, labor, earnings, and love of their forebears.

However, as the mutual-aid system which gave rise to this sense of mutual ownership expanded, it developed flaws. Popes, urged on by archbishops, began to forgive contributors their sins without requiring the acts of penance usually imposed by the Church. More than a few interpreted these "indulgences," as they were called, as open invitations to do as they chose, without regard to morality. They considered their sins forgiven in advance, with the length of time indulgences were good for dependent on the size of their gifts. The trading of indulgences for gifts had much to do with bringing on the Reformation two centuries later. The practice was a main target for the protest of the reformers who founded the Protestant Church.

A second abuse in the mutual-aid system was the waiving of jail sentences, even death sentences, for convicted criminals who agreed to volunteer their labor. Since there was always a cathedral going up somewhere and there was almost always a shortage of labor to build it, smart criminals could easily figure out how to beat their sentences. Actually, they did so at great risk, often merely exchanging one way of dying for another, since cathedral building was hazardous work. The only scaffolds were the rising walls themselves. They had to be scaled. Some of the scaling was done by inclining boards against the walls, some by chiseling out ledges and fitting into them platforms just big enough for a man to stand on. The platforms were connected by crude ladders. But neither device was very safe. The boards slipped. The platforms collapsed. Men were disabled or killed.

Still a third irregularity in the system was the custom of granting all workmen immunity from arrest for the duration of the job. In theory, the Master, or contractor, was responsible for the good behavior of his men, but in practice he would wink at almost any crime as long as a man did his work satisfactorily. As a result, gangs of pickpockets, lock pickers, forgers, and gambling cheats migrated from cathedral building site to cathedral building site, milking innocent citizens without fear of punishment.

By the time the new Reims was completed, it had suffered its full share of the common ills that usually accompanied building—along with one that was unique. About the beginning of the thirteenth century, the Cathedral Council initiated a method of raising money which was thereafter widely copied elsewhere. The council and the Archbishop assembled a select group of citizens and clergy. The Archbishop trained this group in the art of begging, armed them with relics of saints and a letter of introduction from the Pope, and sent them forth as pilgrims. Escorted to the city gates by clergy and people, the pilgrims departed with fanfare. At every church they reached, they set up an outdoor pulpit and harangued the gathering crowds as they had been taught to do. Then they passed the alms basket.

The first pilgrimages were highly successful, but as enthusiasm for them grew, degeneration set in. With no cause but their own pockets, pretenders organized pilgrimages and spent the proceeds. Even legitimate pilgrims were not above overcharging for their "expenses," so that profits declined. Brawls broke out when two or more groups arrived simultaneously at the same church. Whose territory was it?

In 1233 a pilgrimage from Reims, composed largely of clergy, got into a brawl with a pilgrimage from Laon over the right to harangue the parish of Craonne. Craonne, which lay halfway between the two towns, had suffered mass excommunication by the Bishop of Laon for rebelling against his authority. This meant that no one in town could be baptized, confirmed, married, or buried by the Church, or receive Communion. The Laon fund raisers had been authorized to offer the lifting of this ban in return for contributions. But the Remois had arrived on the scene ahead of the Laonnais. Already, they had opened the closed church and set its bells to ringing. In the ensuing battle, Reims lost. The pilgrims returned empty-handed, except for a substantial bill for expenses.

The citizenry of Reims, led by their aldermen, refused to pay the bill. Whereupon the Archbishop, Henri de Dreux, threatened to excommunicate them. In return, the Remois imposed a kind of economic boycott on the cathedral clergy.

Shops refused to sell to them. Tenants moved out of houses rented from them. A few angry burghers went still further; they beat the clergy up. Exasperated and helpless, most of the priests left town. The Archbishop fled to a nearby castle which he owned. It appeared that the town, after its own fashion, had excommunicated the clergy! The Pope tried to intervene as arbitrator, but the Remois told him to mind his own business. They laid siege to the Archbishop's castle, using as weapons building blocks intended for the cathedral.

It took the King of France himself to settle the dispute. The quarrel had gone on for five years when Louis IX, beloved of his subjects and canonized for his piety, persuaded the Remois to listen to him. They agreed to pay for the damage they had done, the amount to be determined by a commission of judges appointed by the King. The judges came up with the sum of ten thousand livres (the equivalent of about $26,000) payable quarterly over a three-year period.

The first payment was turned over promptly to agents of the King. Agents of the Archbishop came for the second collection. It fell due at a time when there had been a bad slump in the wool-weaving business on which more than half the town depended for livelihood. Not everyone was able to meet immediately his share of the levy. Consequently, the payment was incomplete. The aldermen asked for an extension of time in order to raise what was still owing. The collectors refused the request and began to sack houses to make up for the deficiency. Homeowners attacked the Archbishop's men with shovels, picks, stones, bare fists.

In short order the Archbishop himself arrived in the town square, accompanied by soldiers. He excommunicated all citizens, ordered the arrest of the aldermen, the sacking of all houses, and the exiling of many distinguished burghers. The feud was on again. It lasted for two more years until, fortunately for cathedral and people, Henri de Dreux died. The Cathedral Council promptly made amends for Dreux's highhandedness. The excommunication ban was lifted; exiles were recalled, prisoners freed, and damages paid to those whose homes had been looted. The Remois payments still owing were canceled. However, the council also insisted that the aldermen must march barefoot through town, clad only in shirts, while being whipped and repeating, "It is thus that we repay the injury we have done to the cathedral of Reims by stealing its stones." The reference was to the building blocks used in the attack on the Archbishop's castle. It was tolerable to attack the Archbishop but not the cathedral.

During the period of the clash, the building of the cathedral had come to a virtual standstill. It was now resumed with new vigor.

III

The Cathedral Comes of Age

The architect in charge when work on the cathedral was resumed was Jean le Loup. He had served as an apprentice to d'Orbais before taking over himself. In those days architects learned by doing; there were no architectural schools. Jean d'Orbais had learned his trade by serving a standard five-year apprenticeship on the construction of a small church in Reims. Then he trained Le Loup on the cathedral.

There are no records of the personal lives, the dreams, struggles, frustrations, and triumphs of these men. Beyond their names, and the churches which were their handiwork, and in some cases their birthdates and birthplaces, nothing is known of them. Nothing and everything. The everything is Reims. That cathedral reminds us that each of its architects was superb at his craft and devoid of jealousy of the others. Each contributed to the total harmony rather than seeking to impress his own trademark on what had come before. These were men with a mission. Their responsibilities were many, for they were the top bosses of the project. The material returns were low. Any barge captain on the Marne earned more than an architect of Reims.

The architect and his family lived on the work site, often

in a corner of the workshop, which also sheltered tools and twelve to twenty other members of the building crew. In addition to a small salary, paid annually, the architect received a daily stipend for expenses. If he fell ill, the stipend stopped until he was able to return to work. His pay, some of which was in goods rather than cash, was tax-exempt. He was given his food (but none for his family), a pair of work gloves, and a mule for transportation. His wife received a dress.

One of his most important responsibilities was checking the quality of the stone to be used. Much of it had to support tremendous weights without cracking or crumbling. On the other hand, some had to be soft enough for sculptors to carve. Color as well as texture was important. One portal could not be arched from pinkish stone and a neighboring one from gray or white. Consequently, the architect accompanied his carters on every trip to the quarry and personally selected the materials. Since Ebban's time three quarries had opened near Reims. One had its own staff of diggers; in the other two, cathedral workmen had to do the digging. Either way, the architect looked sharply at every piece of stone before he paid for it.

Under him served the Master, or contractor. The Master was assisted by a *parlier*, who was, in effect, an arbitrator between management and labor. His job was to report on workmen's needs to the Master and to interpret to the workers the "musts" of the Master. It was not a job to be envied; the life of a parlier had many a headache. The *compagnons*, the nickname for the workmen, were a tough breed.

They knew full well they were hard to come by. They also knew they were engaged in dangerous work. They were not about to be persuaded to work any faster or take any more risks than they considered necessary. Never mind what the Master wanted. But it was the Master, not the compagnons, who hired and fired parliers. Hanging on to his job while keeping the work force in line required from the parlier the skill of a magician.

In addition to the parlier, the Master, and the architect, there were six other construction executives: a chief carpenter, chief stained-glass craftsman, chief leadworker, chief mason, chief sculptor, and chief locksmith. With the exception of the sculptor, who worked only for the architect, all these chiefs reported to both architect and Master. This double boss system often caused misunderstandings which gave the parlier fresh headaches. The compagnons were responsible to this set of six supervisors, according to trade. That is, locksmiths were supervised by the chief locksmith, carpenters by the chief carpenter, and so on.

The sculptors, appropriately called *ymagiers,* or image-makers, were different. They were a free-wheeling lot. They did not and would not take detailed instructions from anybody. They were required to observe only two rules. First, they had to stick to the general themes—for example, the Crucifixion, the Nativity—given the master ymagier by the architect. The master ymagier generally reserved for himself the most difficult subjects, or shared them with his most gifted men. Then he let the rest of his crew draw lots to determine what subject each would handle. The second requirement was that the sculpture must fit into the allotted spaces. This limitation could prove irksome to an ymagier who was fired with the urge to throw a lion into his scene and was given only enough space for a rabbit. Equally irked were those sculptors whose statues had to serve as supports for rising tiers of galleries on exterior walls. This meant that massive figures had to be hewed from resistant material in proportions precisely calculated to carry given weights. The sculptor full of enthusiasm for airy angels with fluted wings, whose lot assigned him to construct a supportive statue, simply had to deny his creative urge. It was fortunate for the parlier that the sculptors were out of his bailiwick.

The workday for everybody, regardless of task or rank, was dawn to dusk, with an hour off for lunch. In winter there was a fifteen-minute afternoon break for wine; in summer there were two breaks, morning and afternoon, of thirty minutes each. Sunday was the weekly day off. An occasional Saturday afternoon was also granted if the architect was satisfied with the progress and the parlier had persuaded the Master to approach him. All major religious holidays were work-free.

The average pay for the ordinary compagnon was four deniers (the equivalent of about four cents) per hour in winter, five in summer, when sun could add sweat to other complications of the job. After the year 1350 salaries rose to six deniers in summer, five in winter. Midpoint in the fourteenth century a disease called the "Black Death," from the color it turned the blood of victims, rampaged through

Europe, cutting the population in half. Labor became scarce in all trades. One had to bid for it and the laborer worked for the highest bidder.

For a time there were very few prison inmates, formerly an important labor source for cathedral building. In crowded jails the contagion wiped them out. Forced to compete in the open market, cathedrals had to bid high.

The work was dangerous, and inadequate equipment magnified hazards and problems. Block on block, every stone had to be positioned manually, from ground to spire tip. There were crude levers and hand-cranked winches to lift stone to the heights, but from that point on, human hands took over. Masons mixed cement with trowels and hoes. Hammers, bevels, and plumb lines existed, but in short supply. They were usually passed from one section of the building to the next, as needed. Up until 1174, sculptors had used pickaxes, having no chisels.

Understandably, the work moved slowly, but help came in 1240. In order to make possible the purchase of more and better tools and the hiring of more and better labor, the Pope dedicated the decade of the 1240's to helping Reims. From all Christendom he demanded contributions to speed the work. Country fairs donated percentages of their profits; kings and queens emptied coffers; the pious poor gave their pittances. Tradesmen's guilds dipped into their treasuries. Five hundred prostitutes of Paris formed a group which gave the cathedral a munificent sum made up of a week's income from each member.

The Reims workshop hummed with what a cathedral clerk called *"une collaboration joyeuse,"* a joyful working together. At the beginning of the decade, in 1241, the choir space and the rounded apse behind it were completed. The Cathedral Council dedicated the section with fanfare. Already, a third architect, Gaucher, a native of Reims, had been retained and was at work with Jean le Loup. In 1247, when Jean le Loup moved on to a new job, Gaucher de Reims became top architect. It was he who conceived— perhaps as a reflection of the *collaboration joyeuse*—the cathedral's laughter and smiles. He ordered from the master ymagier a group representing the announcement to the Virgin Mary that she was to be the mother of Christ, with Gabriel, the announcing angel, on the verge of a carillon of laughter for the joy of his errand.*

Under Gaucher, the whole style of cathedral statuary began to change. Previously the figures had been stiff. Their clothing, copied from the carved togas of statues left in Reims by the Romans, seemed cemented to their bodies. Their faces were expressionless. The face of Nicaise's sister, Eutropie, for example, is completely bland. Yet this woman is supposedly engaged in the savage act of tearing out a man's eyeballs! The rigidity and lifelessness was due partly to lack of adequate tools, partly to lack of skill. A third reason was the difficulty of making a statue lifelike while

---

* As indicated earlier, many of the Reims angels smile. The original Gabriel was later wrongly placed and now stands next to St. Nicaise at the left door.

at the same time using it as a structural support. Gaucher put an end to this latter practice, thereby freeing his ymagiers from architectural restrictions.

The ymagiers took full advantage of their new freedom. They rippled the garments of their statues in flowing folds, as if of chiffon. They made the figures stand away from the walls instead of backing up against them. Some statues sat. Others bent. The hands were flexed in appropriate activity. In one glance at these statues, the Gaucher touch is instantly clear. See how this king, seated on a cushioned stool, holds his scepter loosely in his right hand, while with his left he fastens his cloak. He is obviously about to rise and leave the throne room. Look at this bearded senior citizen of the Old Testament taking a catnap, his head leaning surreptitiously on his right hand.

The most fluid of all groups is a set of twenty-nine men and women over the left-hand door of the north portal. The scene is Judgment Day, and the twenty-nine are climbing, nude or scantily draped, from their coffins. Some have thrown one leg over the edge; some sit on the edge, swinging their feet; others push up lids. Their glee in emerging from cramped quarters is expressed in every stretching muscle.

Gaucher's fluent style was much admired and widely copied throughout Europe. The statues of the Virgin and her cousin, St. Elizabeth, for example, which stand on the right-hand side of the cathedral's main door, were duplicated precisely in the cathedral of Bamberg, Germany, some forty years after they had been set in place at Reims. Copies of other Reims sculptures of the 1240's were made in Bad Wimpfen, Germany; Salisbury, England; and elsewhere.

A third note in Reims statuary was introduced when Bernard de Soissons took over as architect in 1255. He employed almost exclusively ymagiers born in and around Reims. The result was that the sculpture began to reflect the life of that countryside. On a column head two harvesters fight over a basket of grapes. In a frieze, Adam cultivates the soil of the Garden of Eden while Eve knits. Abel, their son, herds sheep. Cain, their other son, who slew Abel, is, symbolically, a butcher. Over the jamb of the main door a group of carvings shows seasonal occupations: trimming vines in April, haying in July, cutting wheat in August, winnowing it in September, slaughtering a pig for Christmas in December.

Not only the occupations but also the landscape and wildlife of the countryside show up in sculpture of the Bernard de Soissons period. Garlanding the column heads or ornamenting the doors are ivy leaves, pumpkins, strawberry plants, larks, and cuckoos. Vineyards and woodlands, plane trees and swamplands form backgrounds for Biblical scenes. Intended to be a storybook in stone as the windows were in glass, the sculpture of Reims began, under Bernard de Soissons, to speak a language familiar to the people. Louis Gilet, the French art historian, has described the impact: "The cathedral breathed and lived with the people. They talked to each other; they understood each other, they loved each other."

No doubt in Bernard de Soissons's time the naturalistic gargoyles of contented men and animals drew as many responding smiles from congregations as they do today. It was during his term as architect that these drolleries began to enliven Reims's cornices. Oddly enough, they seem quite at home with more serious statues. The fact is that the three periods of sculpture—the primitive, the flowing, the naturalistic—harmonize rather than clash. Comprising 2,300 major statues and probably as many more minute carvings, the three styles exist comfortably side by side. Each piece seems to belong, to be necessary to the life of the cathedral and its people, just as successive stages of growing up are necessary in human life.

The nave of the cathedral, on which Jean d'Orbais, Jean le Loup, Gaucher de Reims, and Bernard de Soissons worked successively, contained, until 1778, a labyrinth, or maze, in the four corners of which their likenesses appeared. In the center was a picture of Archbishop Aubri of Humbert, under whom the building of the Gothic cathedral was begun. The maze, marked out on the floor, was intended for the use of penitent sinners. They followed its intricate pattern on their knees.

Four centuries later, in 1788, a canon of the cathedral, Jean Jacquemart, donated funds to have the maze wiped out. The labyrinth's original purpose had disintegrated; parishioners still tried to crawl in and out of the tangled crisscross, but as a game rather than as a penance. A spirit of revolution was then steaming in the land; it would erupt in another year, and with it contempt for the formalities of the faith. The make-light attitude of the eighteenth-century maze-crawlers was obnoxious to the cathedral staff. They thanked Jacquemart profusely for doing away with this thorn in their flesh.

Pictures of the maze which appeared in old publications prior to its destruction have been preserved by the French National Library. From these we know that inscriptions gave information about the architects' activities. But time has so faded prints and texts that only small bits of the inscriptions can be deciphered. With the wiping out of the labyrinth went all hope of satisfying curiosity about the men whose memorial is the cathedral of Reims. Jean Jacquemart may have served his colleagues well—but his act was a disservice to future generations.

After Bernard de Soissons, an architect named Adam seems briefly to have directed construction. He was followed by Robert de Coucy and, in 1328, by a man called Colard. Ten years after Colard took over, the Hundred Years' War broke out between France and England. The building of the cathedral came to a dead stop for twenty years and after that resumed only intermittently, during periods of lull in the war. The names of two architects are associated with these spurts of activity: Gilles and Jean de Dijon. But the same war that slowed down the work on Reims provided a compensation. Toward the end it brought the still-unfinished cathedral France's most triumphant coronation. To join in that triumph, we must relive some of the

struggle for the French throne which was the cause of the
Hundred Years' War.

The roots went deep—way back to William the Conqueror's takeover of England. When he acquired the
English crown, he held on to his dukedom in France. His
grandson, Henry Plantagenet, married the richest heiress
in medieval France, Eleanor of Aquitaine. The French
landholdings which Henry inherited from his grandfather,
plus others which he took by force, when combined with
Eleanor's, made him master of more than half of France.
He and the kings of England who followed him kept watchful eyes on the other half. Could they grab it? They could
try. Several of their attempts were repulsed. Then, in 1346,
on the battlefield of Crécy, not far from Reims, Edward
III of England, the great-great-great-grandson of Henry
and Eleanor, defeated the French King, Philip VI.

Edward declared himself King of France and England,
but he couldn't make the French half of the title a reality.
The fighting continued, with the tides of war swinging back
and forth between the French and the English until 1415.
In that year Henry V of England led ten thousand men to
a spectacular victory over three times as many French at
Agincourt in northern France. After Agincourt the English
fought their way south until they had conquered all the
French lands above the Loire River. In 1420, having married the King of France's daughter, the victor of Agincourt
was named heir to the French throne. Two years later he

and the French King both died, almost simultaneously. Henry's ten-month-old son was proclaimed "by the Grace of God King of England and France." From Paris an English duke ruled as regent for the infant king.

The Frenchman who, in the normal course of affairs, would have become King of France, the Dauphin or Crown Prince, Charles, secluded himself within the ramparts of Chinon, a redoubtable castle on a rugged cliff overlooking the Vienne River, just south of the Loire. Weak, timid, and tortured by fears that he might be illegitimate (his mother's reputation was notorious), Charles lacked strength and initiative to fight for his throne. He simply pretended there were no problems.

Meanwhile, his country was in a state of chaos. Bands of brigands sold their services as soldiers to the English, to the Burgundians, who were French allies of the English, or to whoever offered the highest pay. Those who could find no offers looted. There was no civil government, not even protection from wild beasts, let alone from brigands. Wolves howled in city streets. The ruling English did nothing to bring about order. Anarchy suited them well. It was to their advantage that France should fall apart by itself. Only a miracle, whispered the terrorized people, could ever save their land.

The miracle came.

It unfolded in a most unlikely way; for several years only a handful of people in a village that consisted of a few houses and a church along a winding lane knew what was going on. Even they didn't understand what transpired.

In this village one bright noontime of early summer, 1425, a thirteen-year-old girl rose from her spinning wheel and stepped out into the yard of her home at the end of the lane. As she leaned against the trunk of an ancient oak, something happened that changed her life and the history of France and England. The event is best described in her own words: "I heard a voice coming as from God. It was a noble voice. It told me to live purely, to pray deeply, to go regularly to church. I was frightened."

At first the girl told no one what she had heard. She was frightened not only of the voice but of what people in the village might think of one who claimed to have heard it. The voice returned. It became voices. The voices became embodied. St. Michael, St. Catherine, and St. Margaret appeared to her, all with the same message: she must "go to France." Go to France was an expression any country girl of her time would have understood. It meant a rare move—leaving the region of one's birth.

Gradually the saints unfolded her destiny. She was to gather an army, drive the English from France, and have the Dauphin crowned King at Reims. *She?* This farm girl who could barely read and who could write her own name only if her hand were guided? Yes, she was a skilled spinner—and a faithful shepherdess too. But were *these* the qualifications for defying the English and crowning a king? Her parents, in whom she finally confided, scolded her. Villagers mocked her. She doubted herself.

Her saints brushed all her objections aside. In February 1429, this farm girl, with an escort of six soldiers whom she had wheedled from a local military governor, set out on horseback for Chinon. She traveled through English-held territory under cover of night, twenty-eight miles a night, a stiff pace for both horses and riders. She had never ridden horseback before.

At Chinon she took lodging at an inn and sent word of her arrival to the Dauphin. News of her approach had preceded her. The Dauphin marveled that she had reached him through enemy lines. He agreed promptly to receive her, but decided on a trick to test her powers. He exchanged clothing with a courtier and set the courtier on his dais, while he himself hid among his nobles.

The summoned girl paused at the threshold of the great chamber. Then, without glancing toward the dais, she made her way through the gathering to the Dauphin and knelt. She said, "Gentle Dauphin, my name is Joan of Arc. The King of Heaven sends word by me that you will be anointed and crowned in the city of Reims and you will be the lieutenant of the King of Heaven, who is the King of France."

Two months passed before the Dauphin gave Joan the army her saints told her she must lead against the English. With it, she drove the invaders from all their strongholds along the Loire River and marched northward to free Reims.

On July 15, 1429, Joan and the Dauphin arrived in Saulx from Chinon. The village of Saulx was not far from Reims. The aldermen of Reims came there to present Charles with the keys to their city. In return, he pardoned all the Remois who had been forced at sword's point to collaborate with the English. The following evening Charles, Joan, and the aldermen, accompanied by soldiers, clergy, and nobles, set out cautiously for Reims. North of the city, the English were still strong, but the little band entered Reims safely by the south gate. As they arrived, the few English and Burgundians remaining in Reims beat a hasty exit out the north gate.

Despite the cordiality of the aldermen, the Remois were not ready for Charles's coronation. Joan's audacity in bringing him there with the English and Burgundians so close by astounded them. They were frightened of reprisal. But love of tradition conquered fear of attack. They lodged the Dauphin in the Archbishop's palace and worked all night long to prepare for a 9 a.m. coronation. By dawn the streets were a-flutter with flags and draperies. Trumpets had been tuned. Birds had been gathered to release from the vaulted ceiling of the cathedral. The sword, scepter, and crown of Charlemagne had been polished to rainbow brilliance.

Joan, meanwhile, prayed and rested at a local inn, L'Âne Rayé, the Striped Donkey. She was joined there by her father, her brother Pierre, and another relative, Durand Laxart, no longer scoffing and scolding. They were proud of her now.

The consecration and coronation ceremonies lasted until two in the afternoon. Through them all, Joan, with a white tunic slipped over her battle armor, stood at the altar near Charles. When the Duke of Albret, acting as High Marshal, pointed Charlemagne's sword heavenward, Joan lifted her banner also and held it high. This was the banner she had carried into every battle. Pennant-shaped, with fleurs-de-lis embroidered on a white background from the center to the forked end, it bore, on the staff end, a portrait of Christ with an angel kneeling to His left, another to His right. Later, when the Burgundians captured Joan and handed her over to the English, she was asked at a Church-conducted trial why she dared to make her banner part of the consecration. She replied, "*Il avait été à la peine, c'était bien raison qu'il fut à l'honneur.*" It had suffered the struggle, that was sufficient reason for it to have shared the honor.

In only one respect was the coronation incomplete. When the Archbishop called the roll of the dukes of the realm to voice acceptance of the monarch, hollow silence followed the reading of the name of the Duke of Burgundy. He was absent, already laying the web that would soon snare Joan. At the finale, when trumpets sounded, Joan threw herself, sobbing, at the feet of the new King. "Gentle King," she said, controlling her tears, "now has the will of God been executed."

Throughout, her face had been grave. Amid all the smiling angels, her lips turned down. Why? Though only an untutored teenager she had singlehandedly succeeded in crowning a French monarch—and that against the armed will of the allied forces of England and Burgundy. Why, then, the melancholy? Because she *was* a teenager. Because she wanted to go home to her family in the house at the end of the lane. She missed her friends, she preferred her sheep and her spinning to the bloodshed in the battles she led, battles in which she used her own sword like a club, only to whack, never to kill. "I wish," she said, at the feast held after the coronation, "that it might please God, my Creator, for me to lay aside my arms and go to watch my sheep." But the English were not yet driven from France.

In the sanctuary of the Reims cathedral today, there is a statue of Joan, grave-faced, helmeted, armored beneath her tunic, her banner unfurled behind her. She looks much as she must have on July 17, 1429. The statue is never without a spray of flowers at the base: white gladioli perhaps, a few lilies of the valley, or golden gorse. Polls taken by the French Institute of Public Opinion consistently show Joan leading the list of revered national historical figures. Reims was the highpoint of the brief career that won her this eternal esteem.

Annually, in spring or early summer, the Remois set aside two days to celebrate Joan's triumph. The city is decorated to re-create as much as possible the atmosphere of the early fifteenth century. In the cathedral square, medieval dances are performed, medieval songs are sung. The climax is the reenactment of Joan's entrance into Reims with the Dauphin, soldiers, aldermen, clergy, and nobles. She dismounts at the cathedral and, with the Dauphin, is welcomed by the city authorities. Then as many as can, press inside for a solemn Mass. The spectacle, replayed with deep reverence, attracts families from all over France.

In Joan's time, and in the two centuries immediately preceding and following hers, another public ceremony rivaled coronations at Reims as a crowd-catching event. This was the mystery play. Mystery plays had their origin in the eleventh and twelfth centuries in the form of drama inserted into the Mass on certain high holy days, such as Christmas or Easter, or on days set aside to honor saints. At first these playlets were in Latin, the language of the Church, but gradually the players began to mix French with the Latin. They ended by dropping the Latin entirely.

As the spectacles became more intelligible, and also more elaborate, they grew in popularity. People traveled long distances to see them. Professional troupes of actors, many of whom wrote their own scripts, performed on scheduled circuits. By the second half of the thirteenth century, the plays had been moved outdoors to accommodate the crowds of spectators. The cathedral steps were the stage, the cathedral façade the backdrop. Often a single drama lasted for a full week, with a different installment presented daily. The presentations lasted all day, with intermissions for eating.

At Reims, three plays were especially popular. One was the week-long drama of the Crucifixion and Resurrection of Christ, written by Bishop Jean Michel of Angers. When this mystery was performed at Reims in 1490 and again in 1530, it drew audiences from as far away as ninety to a hundred miles. Earlier, in 1431, the *Play of St. Étienne* had drawn crowds almost as heavy. Naturally, the business community of Reims profited from such occasions. The cash boxes of innkeepers, food sellers, trinket vendors, and wine merchants jingled with coins of the realm. Not only did established commerce thrive but a whole new area opened up: provisions for the players. Artists set up studios where theater props and sets and costumes could be rented, thus saving the actors the expense and trouble of toting elaborate equipment with them. Money merchants advanced funds to finance productions. The investment was well worthwhile.

The greatest favorite at Reims was so financed. A specialty of the town, it was played there innumerable times during the fifteenth century. The title was lengthy: *How King Clovis Had Himself Baptized at the Request of His Wife, Clotilda, and How in Baptizing Him, God Sent the Sacred Vial.*

Picture the scene at this popular production. From the wooden grillework of balconies around the square hang linen cloths, sixteen feet wide, ten feet high. On them, painted in red, blue, yellow, orange, and brown are figures of saints, prophets, workers, soldiers, Christ, His disciples, and other Biblical figures. Some of the cloths re-create scenes from mystery plays. Others are fanciful. One shows a group of men and women dancing in a circle in the streets of Jerusalem. A little spotted dog outside the circle is trying to join the dance. Another pictures Christ distributing bread and wine to His disciples, smiling broadly as He does so. In still another He is being crushed by a winepress, while above Him vineyard workers labor to keep the press supplied. In the bottom right-hand corner, monks, assisted by laborers, tend grapevines. In the bottom left-hand corner, the sacred wine is being served.

Ninety-seven more scenes hang around the square in strategic locations, turning the place into a veritable art gallery.*

The cloths have been painted in a Remois workshop at the order of the Cathedral Council. No other town can put on such a display, because the process used to treat and paint these cloths is a secret known only to certain Reims artists. Normally this work of theirs adorns the walls of the town Hospice de Dieu, a Church shelter which cares for the sick, the wounded, the jobless, orphans, and travelers who can't afford to stay at inns. But on this day, as on other festive occasions, the cloths are being used to enliven the holiday spirit. The town burghers know very well that they are an added tourist attraction.

The cathedral square is milling with people and more are arriving by the minute. Here comes a group of noblewomen, riding their horses sidesaddle. The horses—led by grooms— are outfitted with gilded and embroidered harnesses. The women are elegantly coiffed, with veils draped over square headdresses. The flowing sleeves of their gowns and the linings of their fringed cloaks are flower-embroidered.

Next, a band of farm boys and girls half dance their way into the square. The girls wear mid-calf-length skirts, white aprons, and tight bodices with long-sleeved white blouses

---

* Of the original estimated one hundred cloths, painted between 1455 and 1520, twenty-five remain. They hang in the Reims Museum of Fine Arts.

beneath. The boys, in knee-length tunics, wear shallow-crowned, broad-brimmed hats.

Close behind are Benedictine monks from the great Abbey of Orbais. With special permission from their abbot, they have trudged some thirty miles to witness the *Clovis* performance. Their feet are dusty and weary, but their faces under the hoods of their monastic habits are alight with anticipation.

The Count of Champagne arrives from his stronghold, Ervy-le-Châtel. He has been on the road for more than a week, and the lavish plumes piled on top of his flat, round hat have been bedraggled by wind and rain. His embroidered velvet cloak is muddy at the hem, and his high-bred horse moves with the pace of a mule. Never mind. He and his retinue of armed retainers are here. The threat of ambush en route has been avoided, thanks to St. Remi and Our Lady of Reims. What he is about to see will well reward him for the hardships of the trip. Before he returns to Ervy, he will repay the good saint and the gentle Virgin for their vigilance by a contribution to the cathedral. He will make a substantial one. May it guarantee a safe journey home.

Through the gathering throng of nobles, peasants, priests, children, burghers, beggars, and bishops, pickpockets glide. They too will profit from this day. In one corner of the square a group of professional gambling cheats lure innocents into their game. In and out of the crowd weave sellers of sweet tarts, their loaded trays suspended by shoulder straps. From wine taverns surrounding the square, laughter rollicks into the street. Business, all kinds of business, is brisk.

Finally the aldermen of Reims arrive. The taverns empty, merriment is hushed. The play is about to begin.

The props and sets have already been put in place. Much of the scene is in miniature. Clovis's symbolic palace, over to the left, is the size of a child's playhouse. Action supposed to take place in the palace will be staged in this area. A tub stands front center. This is the baptismal font. Once jeweled vessels from the cathedral would have been used in the baptismal scene. The first mysteries or *jeux* (literally, games, as they came to be called) relied heavily on cathedral equipment. But in 1373 at Reims the Cathedral Council forbade "any theater troupe" from "borrowing any of the ornaments of the cathedral." Too many were damaged or lost, some said stolen.

However, statues on the façade of the cathedral have roles in the script. Clotilda prays to the statue of the Virgin Mary. Clovis implores victory from a statue of Christ enthroned above the right-hand door. He kneels on the battlefield—a square of green cloth spread out on the paving.

As the actors make entrances from the cathedral, the square is dead still, but the silence is broken from time to time by ripples of laughter. The playwright has included many humorous sallies in his dialogue. Solemn though the subjects of mystery plays were, the authors took good care to relieve the solemnity with wit. Even a Passion play would have some wit about it. The setting for a Passion play, such as Bishop Michel's Crucifixion and Resurrection, was far more elaborate than for any other. On the two occasions when this play was given at Reims, the action took place on a three-level platform constructed in front of the cathedral. The top level was heaven, the middle level earth, and the bottom one was hell. The action was simultaneous in all three.

To the right and left of the platform stood two boxlike wooden towers, in one of which sat God, wearing a golden hat and a scarlet robe. Behind him a stagehand pivoted a giant wheel with angels seated on the spokes. In the opposite tower lived the devil, covered with black tar. Monkeys sat in the wheel behind him. Nearby, a fire burned in an enormous iron pot, around which small devils danced in a frenzy, poking the flames and howling. Far above, Reims's Gallery of Kings looked calmly down on this circus.

Circuslike the plays often were; their writers had shrewdly realized that they needed to be. Especially during the hard times of the Hundred Years' War, they fulfilled a need for escapism, while still carrying the message of the faith. They offered solace in jocular fantasy that nevertheless conveyed a moral. At the same time, Reims's coronations met a different need: their ceremonious dignity was a reminder—through thick and thin—of the nation's heritage.

The king whose coronation followed that of the Dauphin, Charles VII, was Louis XI. Consolidating Joan's victories, he managed, mainly by canny political maneuvers, to bring the Hundred Years' War to an end and to reunite the country. His coronation took place in the spring of 1461, on the day before the Church's celebration of Christ's Ascension to God.

In honor of that celebration, Louis dressed in white damask and rode a white horse. His cloak was red and so were the fleurs-de-lis embroidered on the trappings of his horse. The Archbishop, Jean Juvenal, had ordered the streets over which Louis would pass to be carpeted, and on the carpet, as was the custom at Ascensiontide, the people strewed flowers and sweet-scented herbs.

The clergy in attendance were as distinguished as they were numerous. The Pope sent his legate. The Patriarch of Antioch, who was head of the Church in Mesopotamia and Syria, came in person. Besides Archbishop Juvenal there were four other archbishops, one cardinal, seventeen bishops, seven abbots, and several hundred priests. The nobles of the land were well represented, including the erstwhile rebellious Duke of Burgundy. To him, after the ceremony, the calculating Louis presented his sword and, kneeling, asked the Duke to knight him. At the feast which followed, the flattered Duke showered presents on the King and made all the underlords who commanded Burgundian fiefs swear homage, one by one, to the crown. The roll call allowed the Duke to show off in front of the other nobles the rich array of his estates. It also locked Burgundy back into Louis's kingdom. With this neat arrangement concluded, Louis removed his crown and placed it on the table, a gesture which said plainly to his guests: we are equals.

Louis could be as ruthless as he was cagey. On the day of his coronation, he promised the Remois, as a reward for their welcome, that he would reduce their quota of the tax for the army which all cities had to pay. But in September, when the tax collectors arrived, no reduction was made. Angry argument broke out between the people and the collectors. The argument climaxed in a riot. The collectors were killed and their records burned.

Louis sent soldiers to Reims disguised as merchants. When they had gained entrance to the city, the "merchants" threw off their disguises, drew their swords, and took over the town. The leaders of the riot were banished. Two men and one woman were hanged. One person was quartered alive. Fifty-seven had their right hands cut off. Fifty-eight were fined. Eighty-nine were jailed.

Thus did Louis reward his coronation hosts.

In the time of that monarch the cathedral for which Archbishop Aubri of Humbert had laid the cornerstone in 1211 stood complete except for the spires. They had already been made and the bases for them had been set in place on the tower tops. Before the spires could be mounted, however, certain repairs were needed in the towers. On July 24, 1481, laborers were at work on this job. Two of them had a small firepot over which they heated food. Descending from the roof on some errand, they left the pot, in which coals still glowed. A gust fanned sparks onto the roof. The time was between eleven and twelve in the morning.

A man crossing the cathedral square at that hour saw a tongue of flame dart from one tower. He ran to spread an alarm, but too late. Within minutes the entire top of the cathedral was on fire. The heat rapidly melted the roof's lead base, which "billowed and heaved like a sea in the vaults," according to an account of the day. Hot lead streamed down the walls and spread out over neighboring streets. No one could get near the scene of the disaster. The holocaust could not be halted.

By nine that night the fire seemed to be subsiding. Then suddenly, some spark having found fresh fuel, the flames mounted with new intensity. They raged through the night. Not until dawn did the fire die. Then silently, in the gray light, the Remois gathered to view the damage. They saw that the roof, the central tower, and the galleries around the transept were gone. Much of the statuary, blackened by smoke, masked with lead, was unrecognizable. Their cathedral was a deformed shadow of itself.

IV
Change

At sunup on July 25 the Cathedral Council met. They mapped plans to raise the money to restore Reims. There was no lack of enthusiasm for the task; the Remois not only loved their cathedral, they had become well aware of its value to their community. Nobles and burghers, prelates and priests, guilds and associations of artisans chipped in. Even the beggars who customarily sat at the cathedral portals volunteered to give a tenth of their take to the building fund. There was no need this time for a command from the Pope to put teeth in the fund raising; not even need to send out the usual teams of solicitors. The victories of Joan of Arc, the crowning of the Dauphin, and Louis's reuniting of the French kingdom had solidified reverence for Reims as the shrine of monarchy. Throughout the country, clergy voluntarily took up collections for rebuilding it.

The work began under the direction of Colart le Moine, who had been the architect in charge of erecting the steeples. His steeples were never set in place, however. The cost of rebuilding the basic structure was too great to permit adding frills. The first and most basic job of all was to get rid of the debris. Within a week the rubble had been sufficiently cleared away to permit services to be held. The cathedral was roofless, it was crippled, but it was functioning.

The total replacement of what the fire had consumed took nineteen years, bridging the fifteenth and sixteenth centuries. The last job was reconstructing the multi-statued façade. As the sixteenth century dawned, three masons of Reims, Thierry Noblet, Henry Broy, and Guichart Antoine were engaged to perform this task. The cathedral was almost itself again. Reims, emerging from the Middle Ages, was ready for the Renaissance. To appreciate the impact of the Renaissance on the cathedral's life we must recall the nature of this Europe-wide change in life style.

The Renaissance—though the word, meaning rebirth, is French—began in Italy in the fourteenth century. In the course of four centuries, its impulse toward the bold, the new, the creative moved all Europe. Explorers dared uncharted seas to discover new continents. Artists, architects, writers sought richer and less fettered forms of expression than those commonly considered to be both correct and superior. In Mainz, Germany, a man named Johann Gutenberg invented a printing press. The works of artists and writers could now be more widely distributed. One of the products of the Gutenberg press was a Bible. Formerly, only clergy had had access to the Scriptures. Now any layman with enough money could buy them. He would, of course, have to read Latin to understand what he bought, for that was the language in which the Bible was printed.

Some people began to question why the Bible shouldn't

be translated into the languages they spoke. One of these questioners was a French poet, Clément Marot. He answered his own question by translating the Psalms into French. Marot was among a group of freewheeling thinkers who often met to discuss their ideas in the company of Marguerite of Navarre, sister of France's first Renaissance king, Francis I. Another member of the group was a young student of theology, law, Hebrew, and classical literature, John (in French, Jean) Calvin, later to become the founder of the Presbyterian Church.

As a result of what Marguerite learned from Marot and Calvin, she decided to assemble a circle of court noblemen and noblewomen who would worship God in French, under the guidance of one of Calvin's followers. She was a woman of brains and verve, and she had great influence with her brother, the King. With his agreement, the style which her mode of worship started spread across the land.

As it did so, it began to break more and more with the time-honored dogma of the Church. A year after Francis's coronation at Reims, the German monk-priest, Martin Luther, had begun his campaign against the granting of indulgences in return for contributions to Church work. The campaign attracted many sympathizers in France. The spirit of the Renaissance was beaming a critical light on contemporary concepts and practices of Christianity.

The light put Francis in a predicament. He was attempting to arrange a marriage for his son with a rich Italian banker's daughter. She was a relative of the Pope and the Pope took a dim view of permitting an alliance with a family that supported proposals for religious reform. Furthermore, the *parlement*, which was the high court of the French government, objected to any break with what had become traditional in medieval religion.

So Francis did an about-face. Previously protective of his sister's experiments and the popularity they had achieved, he had Marot jailed. Calvin, threatened with being burned alive, fled to Switzerland. The reformers' form of worship was banned. A royal decree declared that any who disobeyed the ban were to be roasted alive over a slow fire. The reformists, or Protestants, didn't give up. They mobilized; they fought back. They walled cities and defied the government to attack them. They sortied from within the walls to vandalize churches and cathedrals. In an effort to subdue the rebels, government and Church resorted to massacres. The result of Francis's about-face on his policy of freedom of worship was a century and a half of bitter and bloody religious warfare that shattered France.

And Reims? As the bloodshed mounted, Reims had a young, broad-minded, and highly intelligent archbishop to thank for allowing it to escape most of the havoc. The Archbishop, consecrated at the age of twenty-two, was Charles of Lorraine. Besides brains, he had influence. He was related to the Guises, a powerful Catholic family, Church traditionalists, who, in effect, were ruling most of the northern half of the country and terrorizing as much of the rest of it as they could. The Archbishop drew upon his influence to protect reformists' right to peaceful protest in Reims. The result was much haranguing outside the cathedral and little damage inside, except for turning crosses upside down. Once paint was splashed on the altar; once a lantern before a statue of the Virgin was smashed. That was all.

Charles was also a patron and protector of the arts. These, too, were in difficulties as passions kindled in the religious wars. Writers were particularly suspect. If they attacked the established order, their books were banned; often they were imprisoned or exiled. When he could, Charles intervened on the side of freedom of expression. To him, the French and the world owe publication of two Renaissance masterpieces: Rabelais's *Pantagruel* and Ronsard's *Discours des Misères de Ce Temps,* Discourse on the Miseries of This Time.

Rabelais was a satirist. Using his gift for uproarious mockery, he created two characters, a roistering giant, Gargantua, and the giant's son, Pantagruel. In their adventures these two hold up to ridicule all the pretensions of Rabelais's time. One, which Pantagruel exposes, is the hypocrisy of monks who refused to concern themselves with the troubles of their world, at the same time neglecting to practice the faith which was their excuse for withdrawing from it. Rabelais had himself been a monk, as well as a doctor and lawyer.

Ronsard, a lyrical poet, had been a schoolmate of the Archbishop's. He was a devout Catholic; also a thinking Catholic who stalwartly opposed religious persecution. Appalled at the slaughter and destruction which were engulfing his country, Ronsard wrote with burning scorn of the Pope "swollen with riches," while refugee farmers fled from the countryside which the Pope had given to the Guise family. One of the poems in Ronsard's *Discours* describes a farmer "leading in tears his cows by the horns," while another "carries on his shoulders his children and bed."

It is easy to see why, given the temper of the times, the establishment banned both Ronsard's *Discours* and Rabelais's *Pantagruel*. Only a Charles of Lorraine could have succeeded in having the ban lifted. He believed—as he wrote in applying for the revocation—that "education and exposure—not arms and suppression—are the tools with which to fight heresy." Practicing what he preached, he founded the University of Reims, which became one of the great cultural centers of Renaissance France. On the shelves of its library could be found the works of Ronsard and Rabelais, the poetry of Marot, the writings of Calvin and Luther, indeed all the newest in Renaissance literature from all nations. These were shelved with the best of the old, alongside standard Latin texts on the nature and obligations of the Catholic faith.

Charles's enlightened and benign policy paid Reims dividends of peace. When, on August 24, 1572, some fourteen thousand reformists were massacred throughout the country, there were two deaths in Reims. The business community, though predominantly Catholic, was not interested in slaughtering Protestant customers—which many of the university students were. For these students, the university was a haven of both learning and protection.

The August massacre in 1572 had been arranged largely by Henry, Duke of Guise. It triggered civil war. A separate Protestant state was set up in the south under Henry of

Navarre. In the north, Henry III was king, but the actual power was held by Henry of Guise. The contest between the three Henrys for the whole of France was settled in a fashion typical of the times. King Henry had Henry of Guise murdered. Guise's followers murdered the King. With his rivals eliminated, Henry of Navarre became Henry IV of France, in 1589. But he was not crowned at Reims.

A Protestant, Henry had been excommunicated by the Pope. No Catholic archbishop could legitimately crown him. Furthermore, Henry himself had no interest in the ceremony. He wanted to be in the field with his troops, fighting to subdue northern areas which refused to recognize his right to the throne.

Reims was one of those areas. Members of the Cathedral Council published violent pamphlets opposing him. Their emotion didn't spring solely from religious disagreement. Reims had too long espoused moderation, while the rest of the country massacred, looted, and persecuted, to throw restraint suddenly to the winds. What stung the council to the core was Henry's indifference to the coronation-consecration tradition.

But Reims's huff didn't last long. Henry didn't even have to strike a blow to win the town's allegiance. After some deliberation, he decided to be confirmed as a Catholic, in order to unite the country. "Paris," he is said to have declared, "is worth a Mass." He gave the bishops who prepared him for reception into the Church a hard time, however. A man of keen wit and intellect, he couldn't resist shocking them with such remarks as, "The cult of saints is theological legpulling." Also, he frequently asked questions for which they had no answers. In spite of these difficulties with their royal student, the bishops pronounced him ready in July 1593. Clad in white, he was confirmed at the altar of Saint-Denis on the twenty-fifth of that month, then went to Paris to attend Mass at Notre Dame.

Simultaneously, in the cathedral of Reims, a Te Deum, a hymn praising God, was sung. When Henry rode into the city a few days later, bells rang in every steeple, cannons were fired, and crowds waving white pennants shouted *Vive le Roi!* Long live the King! Reims had regained its sanity.

Sixty-one years and two kings later, Reims held, if not the most important, the most spectacular of its consecrations: the crowning of Henry of Navarre's grandson, the sixteen-year-old Louis XIV. The six-day celebration, lasting from June 3 to June 9, 1654, was an indication of magnificence to come. The reign of Louis XIV is known, because of its brilliant splendor, as the reign of the Sun King. With royal encouragement, theater, painting, poetry, architecture, landscape gardening, costuming—all the graces of life that had been nourished by preceding centuries—blossomed forth together. In the canal-threaded gardens of the mirror-lined, ornate palace which Louis built at Versailles, Molière, Racine, and Corneille—playwrights whose dramas are still presented on world stages—went through the agony of first-night productions before the King and his courtiers. If the King applauded, the women in their jewel-appliquéd gowns and the men in ruffled pantaloons and puffed-sleeved tunics put down the cooling drinks they were sipping and followed suit. The playwright and his play were made.

On some nights, Jean de La Fontaine recited his wickedly satiric rhymed fables. The son of a game and forest warden, La Fontaine knew the crows and larks, foxes and wolves, ants and grasshoppers, in fact most of the animals, birds, and insects of France. A court favorite, he knew the wiles of courtiers. Substituting wildlife characters for human ones, he was able, inoffensively but pointedly, to mock the intrigues of courtiers jockeying for positions of influence with the King.

In a more serious vein, La Fontaine wrote of Reims:

Il n'est cité que je préfère à Reims;
C'est l'ornement et l'honneur de France.

No city is there I prefer to Reims:
The honor and the ornament of France.

Born not far from Reims in Château-Thierry, La Fontaine was thirty-three years old at the time Louis XIV knelt at the cathedral altar to receive the crown of Charlemagne. Some flattering references to the coronation in La Fontaine's later work would indicate that he witnessed it.

A complete record of the event was supplied by Simon Le Gras, a bishop of Soissons who consecrated the King, the archbishopric of Reims being at that time vacant. The account reads like a combination of an opera score and a set of stage directions. It had a precise political purpose, and to bolster that purpose, Le Gras neglected no detail. He included words and music for anthems sung by the choir and the texts of all psalms and prayers. He made such observations as: "two stairways, carpeted in purple velvet, embroidered with gold fleurs-de-lis, led to the throne of the King at the altar. He ascended by one and descended by the other."

This welter of documentation led up to a key paragraph: "The gentlemen of the Cathedral [of Reims] Chapter, having deputized and commissioned the visit of the Bishop and Clergy of Soissons, said that they greatly rejoiced in our safe arrival in the city of Reims to consecrate the King; *as it was proper for us to do, being the dean and superior of the province, our right having evolved* from the vacancy of the Archepiscopal seat." *

Some years later, Le Gras's report was published and widely circulated by his successor in office, Bishop Fabio Brular de Sillery. From all Reims, loud protests immediately exploded. The paragraph about Soissons's right, particularly the portion in italics, made it appear, cried indignant clergy and merchants of Reims, that the privilege of crowning kings had passed from Reims to Soissons. Le Gras had, of course, intended to imply just that.

Learned scholars from the University of Reims pointed out in reply that bishops of Soissons had obliged at coronations on two previous occasions when the archbishopric of Reims had been temporarily vacant. No one had then had the effrontery to claim that this courtesy altered Reims's God-bestowed right to consecrate French monarchs.

---

* Italics are the author's.

At stake were considerable sums of money. A coronation was a real boost to the town economy, especially if the King paid expenses for himself, his family and retinue, as did most kings after the mid-fifteenth century. The spectacle drew crowds of money spenders from all the areas around. It was also a boost to cathedral funds, for the offering taken at a coronation ceremony was always a rich one. The contest between Reims and Soissons to sponsor this event was serious.

In an effort to placate Reims, yet maintain Soissons's position, Bishop Sillery offered to let Reims keep title to the coronation collection. The Cathedral Council promptly replied that Soissons had nothing to say about the collection. Like every other portion of the ceremony, the offering belonged to Reims alone.

Sillery employed a battery of legal talent to argue Soissons's case. Reims argued its own, standing firm on the thesis that no human intervention could change the direction of the Grace of God. The controversy reached the King.

Probably the most autocratic of all France's rulers, Louis XIV viewed the bickering as prejudicial to royal authority. The source of a king's power should be above public question. He opted tersely for Reims. Soissons was silenced.

The slender lad who entered Reims to receive his crown gave no signs of becoming the majestic monarch of Versailles. He was, purely and simply, an adolescent who had been scared to death in his childhood and forcibly separated from his girl friend in his teens. His coronation had been delayed until a rebellion could be quelled. At one point the rebels had forced him to flee from Paris. When he was only ten years old, a crowd of them had burst into his bedroom. They had done him no bodily harm, but they must have left troubled memories. The uncertainties of his childhood may well have contributed to the autocracy of his later years.

When he entered Reims with his mother, Queen Anne, her lover, Cardinal Mazarin, political advisor to the royal family, and his uncle, Gaston, Duke of Orleans, the party was met by the aldermen at the city gates. Not included in the retinue was the Cardinal's niece, the dark-haired beauty with whom Louis was wholeheartedly in love. He had been commanded by his mother and the Cardinal to tell her goodbye. For reasons of state he was to marry the daughter of the King of Spain.

The aldermen approached the young King and presented him with silver keys to the city. Two thousand trumpeters on horseback sent a musical volley into the sky. Cannons fired an accompanying under-rumble. Two thousand Remois on foot cheered.

The royal cortege proceeded directly to the cathedral. The Bishop of Soissons and the cathedral canons, clergy, and council, all wearing cloaks of golden cloth, greeted Louis at the portals. He swore allegiance to them and was escorted inside for a Te Deum. After the service, the King and his party went to their lodgings, Louis to the Archbishop's palace, the others to quarters commandeered for them by the Furriers Guild of Reims, which was in charge of their rooming arrangements. The clergy followed the King to the palace, there to complement his oath to them by swearing equal fealty to him.

The next three days were devoted to religious processions in which the King rode and religious services in which he took part. The services were held not only in the cathedral but in all surrounding abbeys and churches. And then, at last, June 7, the day of coronation. The participants had to be early risers. At three o'clock in the morning the Abbot of Saint-Rémy, seated on horseback with a canopy held over his head by four other riders, set out for the cathedral. With him he bore the sacred vial of oil. Before him walked a band of monks, carrying crosses. At 5 a.m. Louis's mother and uncle entered the church with the Cardinal. At six, Louis was fetched. He reached the cathedral from the palace through a covered gallery built especially for his coronation.

Meanwhile, the assemblage had been seated, the high clergy and nobles on chairs cushioned in violet velvet, the velvet embroidered with gold fleurs-de-lis. Tapestries hung from the galleries. The sanctuary was carpeted with soft, rich-hued rugs from Turkey. The altar cloth, a gift from the King, was white satin, jewel-embroidered. The coronation collection was taken in diamond-studded basins, also the gift of the King.

There were some missing faces and voices. The noble who should have held the sword of Charlemagne had been among the plotters of the rebellion which had postponed the coronation. So had many others who should have replied to the question of whether they would accept this king. Substitutes had been chosen. The lack of nobles was compensated for, however, by crowds of ordinary people. Louis had decreed that they should be permitted to sit in the galleries instead of having to wait outside. They lined up in the wee hours of the morning to get seats. Still, there wasn't room for all of them.

The disappointed ones raised a clamor outside. After some hastily whispered deliberation, vergers, the men in charge of cathedral maintenance, summoned a crew of helpers. Carefully they pried loose the lower panes of the stained-glass windows, permitting those outside to peer in.

The ceremony lasted until noon. During the course of it, the choir sang prayers to sixty saints, asking for long life for the monarch, peace and prosperity for the kingdom, and protection for God's holy Church. The saints called upon at greatest length were those of Reims's earliest days: St. Remi, St. Sixte, St. Eutropie, and St. Nicaise.

Finally the Bishop of Soissons intoned, "May the King live forever," the cathedral doors were opened wide, and 480 birds were released from the towers. The crowds in the galleries and those massed outside roared, "Long live the King!"

Louis and his nobles filed into the great hall of the Archbishop's palace for the feast. After the Bishop of Soissons had said grace, guests were seated by rank at tables for royal family, clergy, nobles, and ambassadors from other lands. On a dais in front of a fireplace, slightly above his guests and railed off from them, the King dined alone. A priest mounted the dais, relieved Louis of Charlemagne's heavy crown, and substituted a lighter jeweled diadem.

The next day Louis reviewed the troops of the city guard. On the final day, June 9, he passed among the sick, laying the palm of his right hand on each invalid's forehead and saying, "May God help you. The King touches you." Equally comforting, perhaps, were the coins which accompanied the blessing. These were distributed by the Captain of the Guard, who followed upon Louis's heels.

Eager as the Remois were for the flow of coins, they could also grumble about the inconveniences attendant on hosting royalty. The furriers were a highhanded lot; they dislocated entire families to make room for the guests. As the residence for Louis's mother, Queen Anne, and his uncle, Duke Gaston, they selected the home of Jean Maillefer, a burgher with five children, the youngest a baby of only a few weeks. Jean was summarily ordered to clear all the furniture out of the house so that the furriers could redecorate it in a fashion suitable for royalty. The Maillefer family was at first allowed to remain in one room of the house, but soon after the Queen and Duke moved in, the furriers told Jean to vacate even that room. Desperate, Jean managed to get himself admitted to the Queen's presence. He poured forth his story and appealed to her for help. The Queen ordered the furriers to give the Maillefers two rooms instead of one and to let them have access to the kitchen.

During the conversation between Jean and the Queen, she learned that the baptism of the new baby and the baptismal feast had perforce been postponed. The Queen requested that the baptism be held, feast and all. She and

Duke Gaston would serve as godparents. It was, of course, impossible for Jean to refuse. The Queen brought her entire court to the feast and the Duke brought many of his friends. Jean Maillefer and his wife had to buy and cook the food. Three tables, each twelve feet long, sagged with the weight of roasts, fish, goose liver, loaves of bread, jam, pastries, cheese, fruit, lemonade, cider, and wine. Dishes, linen, and cutlery were borrowed from twenty relatives of the Maillefers and from as many neighbors. Of course, all who helped had also to be invited, which compounded the supply problem. The royal family paid for the food and presented their new godchild with much gold. But nothing could compensate for the staggering amount of labor. Louis XIV's was a coronation the Maillefers remembered—with mixed feelings—for the rest of their lives.

Another who had mixed feelings was Jean Colbert, son of a Reims textile merchant. Colbert's father had trained him to take over the family business, but the young man chose instead to seek his fortune in Paris. He did well, finding himself work as an accountant on Mazarin's staff. He quickly won favor with the Cardinal, for he turned out to have an exceedingly shrewd head for money matters. At thirty-five, he returned to Reims in Mazarin's cortege for the coronation of Louis. Louis was later to make Colbert his finance minister, even though from the beginning the two argued. Louis was ever the lavish spender; for him there was no tomorrow. Colbert was always the thrifty saver, storing a backlog against bad times.

After the coronation feast, Colbert fired off a memo to

Mazarin in which he referred to the meal as "useless" and said that its sky-high cost (the rough equivalent of $200 per person) gave him "violent indigestion." One of his first acts as finance minister was to draw up a table showing the extent to which the King's spending was running ahead of his revenue. Advising Louis to cut expenses, Colbert wrote: "I entreat Your Majesty to allow me to say that Your Majesty has never consulted his finances to determine his expenditures."

Louis didn't take his minister's advice, but he kept him in office because of the brilliance with which Colbert built up France's foreign trade. He found ready markets abroad for Reims textiles, for tapestries and glass. In return, badly needed silver and gold flowed into France. Despite Louis's recklessness with money, finances stayed on an even keel until Louis revoked an edict, the Edict of Nantes, by which Henry of Navarre had established freedom of religion in the land. A majority of the manufacturers whose products were bringing in foreign revenue were Protestants. They left France for countries where they could worship according to their consciences. Despite Colbert's best efforts, France was on the road to financial ruin.

The young Sun King's sumptuous coronation at Reims was like a red sky in the morning, which according to marine folklore means "sailors take warning." As a result of royal expenses and the flight of the Protestants, Colbert was forced to levy crushing taxes, a practice continued by the finance ministers of Louis XV and XVI. Finally, in 1786, the high court of the realm, by which taxes had to be registered to become valid, balked. The court refused to move until and unless an Estates-General was called and gave consent.

The Estates-General was a parliamentary group which met at the pleasure of the monarch, a pleasure in which no monarch had indulged for 176 years until the flat pocketbook of Louis XVI forced him to convene it. Out of the Estates meeting in 1787 grew a National Assembly, representative of all classes of society. This assembly asked the people of France to list grievances that they wanted redressed. The lists, called *cahiers,* or notebooks, poured in from every part of the kingdom. Though they varied in detail, their common nature reveals itself in a statement contained in the Declaration of the Rights of Man and of the Citizen, which the assembly drew up, based on the cahiers: "Law is the expression of the general will. Every citizen has a right to participate personally or through his representative in its formation."

The King was no longer the law, no longer divine. Joan of Arc's concept of him as God's earthly lieutenant was on its way to the guillotine, the beheading machine invented during the French Revolution. That revolution erupted in 1789. The King, Louis XVI, and his queen, Marie Antoinette, were guillotined. Later, as the revolutionary leaders struggled among themselves for supremacy, many of them and their followers were also guillotined. Terror took over. Not until eighty years later, and after three more revolutions, was the ideal of the Declaration of the Rights of Man and of the Citizen achieved.

Meanwhile, what of Reims, that source through which God's authority was believed to be delegated to French kings? What did the revolution of 1789 do to its prestige, which had grown through the centuries since the time of Clovis?

V

The End of an Era

The date was 23 Frimaire (sleet) in the year II, according to the revolutionary calendar, in which the months were renamed, the days redistributed, and the years renumbered. It was, in fact, December 13, 1793. Reims was preparing for a huge parade to celebrate the formation of a Revolutionary Committee in Charge of Surveillance of Suspects. The committee was the local equivalent of a dreaded arm of government, the National Revolutionary Tribunal Council. But it was the equivalent in name only.

During the year, the National Revolutionary Tribunal Council, together with a National Committee on Public Safety, had been responsible for the guillotining of thousands of French men, women, and children, including the King and Queen. The clanging descent of the guillotine's blade, ending with a sickening thump as heads were severed from necks, had become a familiar sound in the central squares of the major cities of France. In Fructidor (September, fruit month) alone, 25,000 heads had rolled. It wasn't uncommon for whole families, from grandparents to infants, to be hauled to the guillotine because some relative was suspected of harboring "anti-revolutionary" senti-

ments or was an *émigré*. The émigrés were anti-revolution-
ists who had fled the country.

At its borders, as well, France was terror-ridden. There
Austrian, Dutch, British, Spanish, Prussian, and Sardinian
troops, reinforced by French émigrés, were mounting an attack. But had one been a spectator in the cathedral square
in Reims that December morning of 1793, one would not
have guessed at the fears which troubled the rest of France.
Certainly the floats that began to gather in the square at
9 a.m. gave no indication of it. The guillotine was nowhere
to be seen. At the height of the revolutionary terror, it did
clang in Reims, but only twice.

The floats grouped in front of the Temple of Reason,
as the cathedral was called, its new name having been inscribed on the front portal. To the left and right of the portal,
several of the statues on the façade were headless. In the
early months of the revolution, mobs had beheaded statues
wearing crowns. They had also torn from the roof the decora-
tive rows of fleurs-de-lis, the royal symbol. The damage was
mild, really. Elsewhere, priceless and ancient works of art
had been totally destroyed. But Reims, Reims still smiled.

Look at the floats. In this one, pulled by a pair of oxen,
stands an elderly couple. A banner stretched above their heads
reads RESPECT AGED AND MARRIED LOVE. In the next one, a
mother bends over a child in a cradle. Several more young-
sters tug at her apron. Other mothers and children follow
on foot. Two young women carry a standard in front of the
float. It says HOW SWEET IT IS TO BE A MOTHER.

There are seven more *groupes moraux*, moral groups, the

name given to such representations by the revolutionists. The last is an impersonation of the Goddess Reason. Painted on her cart are the words LA SOUVERAINE, the sovereign. Workers of various trades march behind her, each man carrying the tools of his trade.

Oversentimental? Overdone? Of course. Also an ironic way to celebrate founding a committee supposed to be made up of witch hunters. Unlike the Reims surveillance committee, those in most of France conducted trials merely as justifications for murder. But whatever else this procession was, it was infinitely better than the procession of carts carrying victims to the guillotine.

Look again. Men, women, and children alike wear the bonnet of the revolution, a kind of stocking cap. But it is not the usual revolutionary cap consisting of three bands of material, red at the top, white in the middle, blue at the bottom. The Remois are again different. In this town of textiles, they knit their own, solid red wool, with a cockade of the tricolor sewed on one side.

The carts leave the cathedral square, amble through town, and return. A bonfire is lighted. Effigies of three figures are burned. The first is the King of France. Second is the Marquis de Lafayette, a supporter of the principles but not the methods of the revolution. The third is the King of Prussia, whose army is at this moment marching toward Reims. As the flames consume his straw-stuffed likeness, the crowds cheer. Then they move, in orderly fashion, through the portals of the Temple of Reason.

The marble altar at which they gaze as they seat themselves is bare. The gold-filigree trim has been scraped from it, and all the gold and silver vessels used in services have been melted down for money. Cathedral clergy have removed the stained glass containing the figures of kings. They have hidden it, for safety, along with the beautifully carved rood screen. There are no trappings now, none at all. But there is gaunt beauty. Though the rich murals have been painted out of the vaulted ceiling, it still soars with Gothic grace above slender pillars. Columns with garlanded heads supporting fluted arches still guard the choir space and gird the nave.

The people wait soberly. The cathedral waits with them. Finally the service begins. The archbishopric of Reims being vacant, the Bishop of Meaux is in charge. He mounts the pulpit, spreads his arms in welcome, and begins: "In place of the celebrations held here in honor of St. Remi, St. Nicaise, St. Sixte, St. Jeanne,* in place of the consecrations held here in former times, you are offered a celebration dedicated to truth, to justice, to humanity, to all the virtues. Recognize, citizens, if you will, the error of the ways into which you have been plunged in the past; give now to the eternal being the only form of worship which is worthy of him; honor him in practicing the virtues which you celebrated today. Every ten days** let all citizens crowd into the temple of the supreme being, not to sing hymns to Mary,

---

* Joan of Arc.
** The French reads *chaque décadi*. Instead of weeks, the revolutionary calendar assigned three groups of ten days each, called *décades,* to each month. The tenth day, a *décadi,* was a holiday.

who was still a virgin after having had a child, but to pa-
ternal love, maternal tenderness, constancy in marriage,
filial piety. Let parents and children encourage each other
in practice of these virtues."

How far in his cheek was the Bishop's tongue? Was the
reference to Mary sarcastic, or was he restating the doctrine
of the Virgin birth in a fashion that couldn't be criticized by
the anti-religionist revolutionaries? Was his reference to the
traditional saints of Reims equally calculated? We have only
the record of the Bishop's words. Like his listeners on that
December 13 of 1793, we can only try to interpret them.
On one point the Bishop was clear: the Remois should come
to their cathedral at the intervals in the new calendar which
corresponded to the Sundays in the old one.

Prior to this day of celebration, Reims had gone through
some very bad times. Though city and cathedral would
avoid the general terror which was to reach its height in
the rest of the country between 1793 and 1795, the three
previous years, from 1789 to 1792, had already been years
of crisis in Reims. In November 1789, the revolutionary
government decreed that "all ecclesiastical wealth is at the
disposition of the nation." Acting under this decree, the
guilds of Reims got together to decide what should be done
with the cathedral's holdings. These included the revenue
from thirteen parishes, three churches, and a host of well-
endowed abbeys.

The shoemakers' guild suggested that "useful clergy,
such as parish priests and curates, should have their income
improved, while higher officials, of which there are too

many, should have theirs reduced. No religious order should be bigger than forty persons with an average annual income of 700 livres* for each."

Said the printers: "The immense revenues of the Church should be used according to the intentions of the founders of the Church, that is, for the honest and decent support of all clergy necessary to the Church, particularly those who administer parishes. Church money should also be spent to maintain religious buildings in need of repair, rather than enlarging the luxury of great establishments."

The other guilds, except for the tapestry makers, agreed. Unlike the government, which wanted to get its own hands into Church coffers, the Reims guilds wanted Church wealth redistributed within the Church itself. The tapestry makers insisted that "Church wealth should be used to help the state pay its debts." This was what the state intended to do, and did do, in Reims and throughout the country.

At the same time, however, the government, bowing to a majority sentiment in the nation which held with the Reims printers and shoemakers, allocated some of the confiscated Church revenues to pay parish priests. But there was a price. Once the Church became the employee of the state, clergy were required to swear loyalty to the principles of the revolution and the administration in power.

The loyalty oath was the rub. Of Reims's score of priests, only two would swear. The Archbishop fled. The government fired the non-swearers, but a number refused to be

---

* The equivalent of approximately $1,680.

fired. They boldly continued to officiate in the cathedral. They devised all sorts of means of defying government edicts. One foresighted young curé, in charge of the chapel of St. Remi, even managed to preserve for future generations a few drops of the oil from the vial of St. Remi, which the government was determined to destroy. The vial, representing as it did the authority of God and monarch, was the symbol of everything the revolutionaries opposed. So important to them was it to get rid of this national image that a special deputy, one Philippe Ruhl, was dispatched from Paris to Reims to make sure the vial was shattered.

Ruhl made a ceremony out of the shattering. In the cathedral square he took the fragile glass from the young curé and splintered it on the cobbles. A crowd watched. As soon as Ruhl turned away, those in the front lines fell on their hands and knees at a prearranged signal and gathered up as many fragments as they could. The night before, the curé had already extracted and hidden a little of the oil.

The destruction of the vial, together with the question of the loyalty oath, divided Remois opinion down the middle. In 1791 and 1792, seven riots broke out between supporters of the Church, like the printers and shoemakers, who wanted to reform but not abolish religious practices, and supporters of the government, like the tapestry makers, who wanted to substitute government for God.

Meanwhile, in the cathedral, a regional assembly was meeting to choose deputies to a national convention called to write a new constitution for a republic of France. Elected president of Reims's assembly was a moderate man from nearby Châlons, Pierre Louis Prieur. Physical violence was abhorrent to Prieur. He tried to shut his ears to the howls of mobs in the square that frequently interrupted the assembly's deliberations, but he could not. Time and again, he quit the president's chair to go outside and help rescue some victim from the mob. One afternoon he pulled from the clutches of pro-government assailants a priest who had refused to take the loyalty oath. The assailants turned on Prieur and beat him up. Weary and battered, he turned over the presidency of the assembly to Nicolas Diot, a priest who had taken the oath and whom the government had ordered to pinch-hit for the Archbishop.

As Prieur left the meeting, night was falling. He heard scuffles and muffled cries from the gardens behind the cathedral. He investigated. Sixty men had again gotten their hands on the hapless priest he had rescued earlier. Prieur threw himself into the center of the fray. He would have been killed if some young soldiers from troops massed in Reims to defend it from the Austrians had not also been attracted by the noise. They came to Prieur's rescue.

But not all soldiers—there were fifteen thousand of them in Reims—were so helpful. At the same hour that Prieur and the priest were saved by one group, the postmaster of Reims was being murdered by another at the opposite end of town. That night, besides the postmaster, six priests, one noble, and one weaver were massacred.

The next morning all the guilds met. Regardless of their differing political opinions, they agreed that the bloodshed had to stop. The weavers guild, particularly incensed by the murder of one of their members, organized the others. Each guild was assigned a strategic position in which to stand guard. Within a month, the guilds had restored order to Reims. When the terrorists among the revolutionaries took over the national government the next year, blood flowed through France but Reims remained quiet. The Remois had already tasted blood and spat it out. They turned their cathedral into a storehouse for animal feed and let it go at that. Reims sat out the final three years of the revolution.

By 1795, the terrorists had killed each other off. The people were weary and hungry. Transportation had been totally disrupted, as had the system of distribution. The result was that foodstuffs, still in ample evidence in farmers' fields and pastures, were reaching markets only with great difficulty and at very high prices. Meanwhile, new paper money, created in the revolution, supposedly backed by confiscated Church riches, had proven worthless. For the majority, existence was a matter of scrounge as scrounge can. The constitutional convention had come up with a proposal for a Directory of five men, to be elected by a two-chamber assembly, which was in turn elected by the people. Lackadaisically, the people accepted the plan. Some form of law was better than no law.

The Directory, however, proved unable to do anything about hunger, high prices, or worthless money. None of its members was noted for his brains. They had easy access to a flourishing black market and they were happy with the dandified plumes, laces, and silken breeches which were part of their pay. The people called them "rotten bellies."

To distract public attention from its weaknesses, the Directory started wars. In these wars a young man of twenty-eight, who had been born on the outpost French island of Corsica, in the Mediterranean Sea, won fame for himself. He was a brilliant strategist and an ambitious one. Once, after a particularly important victory, he held a reception to which he invited generals and nobles. To the applause which his guests gave him, he replied, over his glass of wine, "What I have done so far is nothing. I am but at the opening of the career I am to follow. Do you think that I have gained my victories in order to advance . . . the Directory? Do you think, either, that my object is to establish a republic? What a notion! What the French want is glory and the satisfaction of their vanity . . . The nation must have a head who is rendered illustrious by glory and not by theories of government . . . or the talk of idealists."

This twenty-eight-year-old had put his sensitive finger on the very core of the French central nervous system. Though he was not speaking of Reims's Clovian tradition, he had perceived the need that tradition had fulfilled for so many centuries. Seven years later, at the age of thirty-five, he revived echoes of Charlemagne's Holy Roman Empire. He maneuvered the French Senate into naming him Emperor. Not at Reims, but at Notre Dame in Paris, he took from the Pope the imperial crown and placed it firmly on his own head. He, Napoleon Bonaparte from Corsica, was now Emperor Napoleon the First of France.

Though he chose to be crowned in the nation's capital,

Napoleon had been careful not to slight Reims. The year before his coronation, while occupying an office with the title of First Consul of France, he made a point of visiting the cathedral city. He arrived at three o'clock on an August morning; despite the hour it was all the city's police could do to clear a way for him through the welcoming crowds who turned out in the pre-dawn blackness. The light of their torches and their cries of *"Vive Bonaparte"* accompanied him from the gates to the cathedral, where he was given the keys to the city and attended Mass. At 9 a.m. he began a round of appointments with town authorities. Not a single person was overlooked, not even the man in charge of repairing roads and bridges. Napoleon's wife, the Empress Josephine, was meanwhile visiting the Hospice de Dieu. Afterward she received twelve schoolgirls, dressed in white and bearing baskets full of presents: eight horns of pears, a dozen loaves of spice bread, goose liver, and other delicacies for which Remois farms and kitchens were famed.

At four-thirty in the afternoon, Napoleon rode through the town streets on horseback, accompanied by sixty foremen of textile factories, organized as a guard of honor. Then he toured the factories. Later the Empress joined him at the cathedral for evening prayers, and the two had a conference with the Archbishop. On to a ball and reception given by the Chamber of Commerce at which the Empress danced the night through. When Napoleon was crowned in Notre Dame, the Archbishop of Reims, accepting an invitation from the Archbishop of Paris to attend, wrote: "With great pleasure will I witness the elevation of the servant of

God whom it has already been our right, our duty, and our privilege to prepare for and confirm in a just defense of the Church and the people."

Eleven years later, in 1814, Napoleon enjoyed at Reims one of the last satisfactions of his high-rocketing, fast-fading career. He had attempted to go Charlemagne one better and conquer all Europe. The result, in his own words: "A year ago all Europe was marching with us; today all Europe is marching against us." Although he did not know it, he was on the eve of being exiled from France.

On February 6, 1814, twenty thousand Germans and Russians marched on Reims. On March 12, the Eighth Corps of the Russian Army occupied the city. The corps was commanded by a French traitor, Emmanuel Saint Priest, leader of a band of sellouts in the region.

At eleven o'clock in the morning on March 13, Saint Priest was attending Mass in the cathedral when a message reached him that Napoleon was approaching Reims with 22,000 soldiers and had sworn to sleep in the city that night. Saint Priest rose hastily from his knees, left the cathedral, rallied his troops, and rushed forth, hoping to block Napoleon's way. The ensuing battle was fought in the hills around Reims. By 2 a.m. on March 14, the Russians had been put to rout, Saint Priest was dead. Napoleon entered Reims.

He remained there through the sixteenth, resting his troops. In front of the cathedral, the townspeople acclaimed him their liberator. In return, Napoleon gave them a show, a *caracoler*, horseback maneuvers. "The good people," says a contemporary account, "swam in joy." Their joy was short-lived. The Russians were soon to retake Reims, not to leave until Napoleon was exiled to the lonely isle of Elba off the coast of Italy in the Tyrrhenian Sea. A monarch, Louis XVIII, was about to return to the throne of France.

In 1821, Louis XVIII having sat temperately and safely on his throne for seven years, Reims held an *Amende Honorable*. The ceremony was intended to make amends for the sins of the revolution, which had cast out monarchy and subverted the faith. It began with a Mass, during which the Archbishop placed himself and his congregation at God's mercy. For the next three weeks a different daily event implored forgiveness. There was a Communion service for women, another for men. There was a renewal for all of the vows which had been taken at baptism. There were candlelight processions around the cathedral and hours of silent devotion before the altar.

There was also an interesting exercise in debate. Daily at noon, on the cathedral steps, two priests debated some of the most baffling questions in Christian doctrine, such as: Was Christ really the Son of God? Was He born of a Virgin? Is there a life after death? One priest purposely and purposively upheld the negative, while his opponent took the affirmative. Of course, the debate had been carefully prepared and rehearsed and the affirmative always won. The argument was in no sense free. Nevertheless, the priests who devised it were wise men. They understood that a contest held more interest for an audience than a sermon. The contest also gave the clergy opportunity to bring up and attempt to remove many of the doubts which they suspected haunted the minds of their parishioners after the revolution. At the end, the *Amende* was climaxed by a procession from the cathedral to a nearby hill, where a giant cross, covered with crimson cloth, was planted at the summit. Thus did the clergy attempt to recommit Reims to its ancient traditions.

But no clock can be made to run backward. Louis XVIII was a moderate man, not given to trying to travel upstream while the currents of history flowed down. Not so his brother Charles, who succeeded to the throne and who had visions of re-creating the glory of the Sun King. His coronation at Reims was symptomatic. Louis had forgone the pomp and ceremony of Reims, but Charles was determined to revive it, resurrecting all the pre-revolutionary symbolism which had characterized so many centuries of French coronations. He sent his royal procurer from Paris to conduct an inquiry into the whereabouts of the splinters of the sacred vial which had been picked up from the cobbles of the cathedral square in 1793. As many as could be located were reassembled into a new vial. The oil which the curé of St. Remi's chapel had hidden was also found and mixed with fresh oil, which was poured into the reconstructed vial—the whole housed in a golden box.

The Archbishop and clergy of the cathedral dug frantically into the archives to inform themselves on a ritual which had not been practiced for fifty years. The Chamber of Commerce offered rewards to town oldsters who could recall specific details of the last coronation, that of the hapless Louis XVI, whose head subsequently rolled from the guillotine. The city was, as the Secretary of the Cham-

ber of Commerce described it in expressive French meta-
phor, *"sens dessus dessous,"* turned upside down, in an effort
to reconstruct the customs of an age gone by.

In addition to Reims's effort, the nation at large was set
to work. Poets and writers, in particular, were called upon
by His Majesty to commemorate the occasion in odes and
essays. There was no lack of available literary talent.
Charles's reign coincided with the beginning of a passionate
style of expression now called Romanticism. It tended to be
lush in verbiage, idealistic in viewpoint, always intense—
and intensely personal. Two of the leaders of this school in
France were the poet Alphonse de Lamartine and the nov-
elist-dramatist-poet, Victor Hugo. Lamartine was commissioned by Charles to compose the verses for a chant sung at
the coronation. Victor Hugo produced 170 sonorous lines
in which he evoked the ghosts of Clovis, St. Remi, Charlemagne, Joan of Arc, St. Louis, and Louis XVI. As for
Charles, Hugo declared him in wisdom and splendor the
equal of King Solomon in the Old Testament of the Bible.
Then, continuing, Hugo added: "Charles receives, without
flinching, this crown, heavy with the weight of the glory
of sixty kings of France."

Toward the end of the ode, Hugo called upon the trumpets to sound forth. "The Prince is on the throne," he wrote,
"enter the cathedral, O people. Like a lighthouse surrounded by waves of the sea, so he shines on the undulant
crowd, while a thousand singers of the air, happy as the
people, mingle their voices and feathers, flying on high."
The singers of the air were, of course, the traditional doves

let loose from the vaulted ceiling at the finale of a coronation. "Behold him, priest and King," Hugo concluded.

The extravagant ode was by no means worthy of the at
once epic and thoughtful writer into whom the author later
matured. However, one verse is an exception to the rest.
In it, Hugo evokes the spirit of the cathedral and its meaning for France.

> *Le vieux pays des Francs, parmi ses métropoles,*
> *Compte une église illustre, ou venaient tous nos rois,*
> *De ce pas triomphant dont tremblent les deux pôles,*
>   *S'humilier devant le croix.*
> *Le peuple en racontait cent prodiges antiques;*
>   *Ce temple a des voûtes gothiques,*
>   *Dont les saints aimaient les détours;*
> *Un séraphin veillait à ses portes fermées;*
> *Et les anges du ciel, quand passaient leurs armées,*
>   *Plantaient leurs drapeaux sur ses tours!*

> *Royal archdiocese, this country of the Franks*
> *Counts you among its glories; church where all our kings*
> *With steps to shake the poles came in triumphant ranks*
>   *To bow before the cross that brings*
> *A hundred memories; wondrous tales the people told*
>   *Of many miracles of old*
>   *Beneath these vaults in Gothic bowers*
> *Beloved of saints, behold—a seraphim stood by*
> *To guard the doors while angel armies from the sky*
>   *Planted their standards on your towers.*

Both Hugo and Lamartine were to become disillusioned with Charles and to play active roles in the revolt which unseated him, as well as in subsequent revolutions through which France struggled and groaned until 1875. Not until then did the country emerge as a republic.

Not all the Romantics were as taken by Charles's coronation as Hugo and Lamartine. In fact, some were forthrightly critical. Chateaubriand, a foremost statesman, historian, poet, and philosopher, called the ceremony "the playing of a consecration, but not a consecration." Sumptuous, correct in every detail, it was glacially artificial. The conviction which had given the ritual warmth and meaning had gone with times gone by. Pierre Jean de Béranger, a popular lyricist, wrote a sarcastic song, "The Consecration of Charles the Simple," which became a national hit. It was sung in cafés and cabarets, in cottages and châteaux, in factories, on farms.

One of the verses went like this:

> *De Charlemagne, en vrai luron,*
> *Dès qu'il a mis le ceinturon,*
> *Charles s'étend sur la poussière.*
> *"Roi!" cri un soldat, "levez-vous!"*
> *"Non," dit l'évêque, et par Saint Pierre,*
> *"Je te couronne, enrichis-nous.*
> *"Ce qui vient de Dieu vient des prêtres.*
> *"Vive la légitimité!"*

> *With Charlemagne's belt securely trussed,*
> *Charles stretches flat upon the dust,*

A monarch clown, king of the show.
"Up, King!" a soldier, shamed, demands;
The Bishop stays him with a "no."
"I'll crown you by Saint Peter's hands—
"Enrich us who hail your legitimacy!
"It comes from God through priests," claims he.

The reference to legitimacy had to do with the weakness of Charles's claim to the throne. Many, including Chateaubriand, believed that the consecration ceremony was resurrected to give the impression that the claim was supported by no less a person than the Deity Himself. Wrote Chateaubriand: "Where legitimacy is entirely missing, it is necessary to bolster it by any and all means, come what may." Others saw the consecration as a bargain between Charles and the higher-ups of the Church. He needed clerical support; the bishops needed his approval to regain status and wealth. This interpretation is also implicit in Béranger's song.

It was equally clear in the after-dinner speeches at the coronation feast. The elderly cardinal chosen to preside, Clermont-Tonnerre, opened by saying, "The august ceremony of the consecration of Your Majesty has spread joy and happiness throughout France. It represents the triumphant return of religion. For the first time in half a century this sacred religion has solemnly consecrated the destinies of France. Your Majesty has regained his heritage. May Your Majesty's wisdom find no obstacle to prevent the carrying out of its purpose: to give the Church of France that kindly protection which is necessary to meet the needs of the people confided to our pastoral care and solicitude."

Charles's reply was cagey: "All that I will do for religion, I will do for the happiness of my people." The Remois tried hard to create the illusion of joy. The town prefect with a crowd met the King at the gate and intoned a set speech: "Sire, you are about to hear the acclamations of the descendants of those who were commanded by Clovis and instructed by St. Remi. They lift their voices to the sky at the sight of the monarch for whom they have been so ardently waiting. I can serve here only as the organ of their impatience, for these cries, this intoxication of a great people, make up the only language which is not in any way beneath the dignity of the King of old France and of the august ceremony which brings him here to us."

The rub was that Charles was not the King of old France, for there was no more old France. Nor was there, as yet, a new France. Despite the impressive gathering of bishops who, with the Archbishop, welcomed Charles on the cathedral steps, he was really only king of a country in a chrysalis.

The cathedral had been thoroughly redecorated for the coronation—and in very bad taste. The richly carved façade was half hidden by an ugly porch, erected to shelter the welcoming bishops and the arriving monarch. To make room in the galleries for expected crowds of notables, all the gallery statues had been removed from their cornices and niches. In a popular journal of the time, *Revue de Deux Mondes* (*Review of Two Worlds*), Victor Hugo wrote: "More damage was done to the cathedral in attempting to . . . refurbish it in time for the coronation than had been done by any of the vandalism of the revolution." Despite having succumbed to the lure of a coronation, Hugo had no sympathy for meddlers with the cathedral architecture.

In the course of the refurbishing, a workman, painting gold stars on the ceiling, fell from his scaffolding and died. From tongue to tongue, news of his death traveled through town. People shook their heads. They considered the accident an evil omen. Whether it was or not, the workman's death coincided with the death of an age in the interlinked history of the country and the cathedral. Charles's coronation was the last at Reims. Six years later he was forced to flee. The Clovian tradition which had made the cathedral a stepping-stone between monarch and God was dead as a political influence.

It was not dead as sentiment, however. The old story of Clovis, Remi, and the founding of the French nation is to this day colorfully narrated by every guide who conducts modern visitors through the cathedral and its precincts. And the boxed bits of sacred vial and drops of oil located for the consecration of Charles are preserved and displayed in the reconstructed Archbishop's palace. In 1972, after twelve years of painstaking research and building, this palace, bombed to the ground in World War I, and left in ruins for more than two generations, was reopened to the public. It was known to the medieval Remois as the Palais de Tau, because of the T-shape of the ninety-foot-long by thirty-three-foot-wide dining hall where the coronation feasts were held. Tau is French for the Greek letter T.

This faithfully restored residence of archbishops and lodging of kings is vibrant with ghosts of the ages. The oak-beamed ceiling of the dining hall arches thirty-three feet above walls covered with blue hangings, on which gold fleurs-de-lis are embroidered. Superimposed on the hangings are tapestries, one hundred feet long by thirty feet wide, depicting, according to their inscriptions, "The History of the Strong King Clovis." At the far end of the room in the crosspiece of the letter T is the fireplace, seven feet high by twelve feet wide. Here was set the monarch's place, so that he might eat "back to the fire, belly to the table," as the fifteenth-century designers of the chamber described their intentions. One can almost see the young Sun King, Louis XIV, successfully crowned after defeating a rebellion, basking here in the pleasant glow of fire and food.

One can imagine also the succession of archbishops kneeling in the austere palace chapel which Jean d'Orbais had designed in the early thirteenth century. Prayers for funds to restore the cathedral when gutted by fire, to protect the cathedral when threatened by fanatics, prayers for safety from the Black Death, from invaders, from drought in the surrounding vineyards, prayers for the health and long life of the monarch and peace for the country must have mounted like incense from this sanctuary. One such prayer, composed by Archbishop Charles of Lorraine, has come down to us. He wrote it during the religious wars of the late six-

teenth century, when attacks by writers on established institutions were being banned and the authors penalized.

> *Thou who art the fountainhead of wisdom and of truth,*
> *restrain us lest we mistake our human judgment for*
> *thy will. Save us from persecution in thy name.*
> *Let us never fear that thy justice will fail. Give us*
> *courage earnestly to seek our own errors rather than*
> *the errors of others. In the name of thy Son and all*
> *thy blessed saints, we ask this grace.*

Everywhere in the palace, treasures recall eras in the life
of the cathedral and the history of France. Here is a talisman
worn by Charlemagne; there a Communion cup from which
St. Louis drank at his consecration. The silver cross and candlesticks on the chapel altar are those used by Napoleon at
his Paris wedding to Marie-Louise of Austria.

In sweeping corridors stand statues dislocated by one or
another of the cathedral's misfortunes and too badly damaged to be returned to their niches. Their original places
are now occupied by reproductions. Despite the damage, the
impact of these originals is powerful. Among them are two
twelve-foot-tall figures, one of Christ, one of St. Thomas.
The trunks of the statues, blackened and mutilated, have
lost their form. But the heads have escaped damage. Both
faces are transfigured by what Jean Feray, chief inspector of
France's historic monuments, has described as "the mystical
Remois smile."

Thus is the heritage of Reims preserved. In the hearts of

the French that heritage satisfies a national desire for what Napoleon defined as *la gloire*, glory. At Reims they possess it still, but no longer does it possess them.

Toward the end of the nineteenth century, France at long last became an organized republic. The cathedral kept pace. Revolutionary damage was repaired and the atrocities committed for Charles's coronation were done away with. Several architects worked on the restoration, but the guiding spirit and most important was Eugène Viollet-le-Duc. A scholar as well as an architect, Viollet-le-Duc had as his professional passion the Gothic style. He studied examples of it throughout Italy and France—and not only the great cathedrals but roadside shrines in remote villages, town halls, façades of shops and houses in crooked old-time streets. He wrote extensively of his findings, illustrating his writings profusely. As a result he was in great demand to supervise work on France's historic Gothic monuments. At Reims, he put the galleries to rights, replaced the rooftop fleurs-de-lis removed by revolutionaries, tore off Charles's grotesque front porch, and uncovered and restored dozens of merry gargoyles. These had been submerged in superstructures imposed on the cathedral through the ages.

As the century turned, the town of Reims was lucky to find in one of its native sons as ardent a student of the medieval art of stained glass as Viollet-le-Duc was of Gothic architecture. The young man's name was Paul Simon. His studies had revealed to him the secret of the deep, gemlike quality of medieval glass as compared with the more superficial coloring of later panes. Whereas the more modern craftsmen worked with panes of equal thickness, the old masters had deliberately selected unequal thicknesses. They placed the thinnest at the center of a window, graduating outward to the thickest at the edges. This technique had two effects. First, it gave the window the appearance of magnifying itself. Second, sunlight penetrated the whole at unequal speeds, giving rise to a glinting play of colors.

Using this method, Simon restored the rose window of Reims splendidly. While he was at work, others repaired the peeling façade between the window and the Gallery of Kings. The cathedral was again becoming the work of joyous collaboration it had been in the thirteenth century. At this point, a great French composer, Claude Achille Debussy, inspired by hours of reverie in the cathedral, wrote his famous piano prelude, *La Cathédrale Engloutie.*

Engloutie means drowned or engulfed. Why did Debussy think of the cathedral in those terms? Far from being engulfed, it was being reborn. Perhaps the answer may be that Debussy himself became engulfed by Reims, drowning his own personality in the personality of the cathedral. He expresses his sense of identification in a powerful yet elusively haunting cascade of musical images.

Images? In *music?* Yes. Claude Debussy was the leader of a group of composers who believed that—to quote him —music should offer listeners "mysterious communion with the winds, the quivering of leaves, the scent of flowers"— or whatever else had inspired its composer. He once described a nocturne he had written as "luminous dusk participating in total rhythm." He felt, as did certain circles of writers and artists of his time, that the function of all art was to provide an impression of subject matter with which the reader, the viewer, the listener, as the case might be, could merge his personality, in the same way the artist had already merged his.

Painters and musicians who shared this belief were called Impressionists. Writers of the school were known as Symbolists. To achieve their aim, all attempted to call simultaneously into play as many of the five senses as possible. A Symbolist poet, Charles Baudelaire, wrote of perfumes, colors, and sounds, replying to each other until they joined in one long echo. His poetry beguiles readers into sensing an echo not only with their ears but with their noses and eyes.

So Debussy wanted listeners to react to his vision of Reims with their ears. Long fascinated with music of the Middle Ages because of what he considered its uncluttered purity, he had already begun to imitate medieval monophonic, that is, chordless style. He had set to music some of the period's best-known poetry. To his reverie at Reims, he brought this background. He also brought his abandonment of old restrictions. For example, though it was customary not to use more than two keys in a single composition, Debussy changed keys whenever he felt the mood he was trying to convey required the change. Sometimes he modulated —that is, changed keys—with every beat during long passages. He preferred dissonance to conventional melody and he utilized it to such advantage that his dissonance seemed to make a melody of its own. With chromatics he was masterful.*

His techniques did not win Debussy quick popularity. *La Cathédrale Engloutie* at first was called "musical anarchy" by critics. But the composer lived to hear his work acclaimed and himself called "Claude de France," because so much of his music is expressive of the deepest French sentiments.

The *Cathédrale* prelude opens with two high, distant notes, repeated. A rumble is heard below them, a ripple above them. Then—to imitate bells—Debussy intersperses his usual monophonic style with chords. Only one bell tolls at first. Then the chords expand to finger-stretching lengths, the bells resound, they din in chorus, with the left hand in the bass supplying deep-throated bongs. The din hushes, gives way to a distant hymn. The hymn swells and subsides. The bells return, loud, but not so loud as before. They soften: a bass gong turns into a sustained rumble. The opening theme of high, sweet notes repeats itself. Four bass notes breathe two Amens.

Has Clovis been baptized? Does light illumine Remi's face? What kings kneel for the crown of Charlemagne? Do

---

* For non-musicians: Western scales consist of seven whole tones and of half-tones between them. From different combinations of these tones and half-tones, forty-three different scales can be constructed. The scale within which a composer chooses to write his piece is known as "the key." The orthodox composer uses only slight variations from the combination of tones and half-tones which define this key. The chromatic scale is keyless. Instead of using only a selection of tones and half-tones, it uses them all.

Joan's tears wash the Dauphin's feet? Does flame burst from the towers? Is that Aubri of Humbert and Jean d'Orbais laying the cornerstone of this cathedral? Choose what images you will. The prelude is your projector, your ears the screen. At the loudest peak, the crescendo of the piece, the impact is majestic. In the gentler hymn, the images are otherworldly. Debussy called his prelude "non-dimensional." Ages pass in its five-minute length. France engulfed has been ably resurrected by Claude de France.

The prelude was written in a period of political and social uncertainty by a man who was as much a political as a musical rebel. In Debussy's France, old standards were changing, new ones were forming but not yet formed. The ordinary Frenchman was questioning authority as he had never done before. Recently organized trade unions were beginning to use strikes as bargaining weapons. Railroad workers, postal clerks, vineyard workers were on the march. A newly alert press and a new breed of crusading journalists were tracking down government graft. An army scandal erupted when an innocent man, Captain Alfred Dreyfus, was convicted for the crime of another. An aroused public won a reversal of the verdict—but only after Dreyfus had spent twelve years in jail. And while these events transpired, some leaders of the old order were scheming to restore the monarchy.

The man who wrote the passionate prelude for Reims wrote equally passionate editorials calling for reform in the face of such developments. Debussy worked as a newspaperman to augment for a while the meager income from his at first unpopular music. The seeming contradiction between his politics and his prelude is easily explained. Regardless of regime, regardless of social climate, Reims remained Reims, remained France—whatever kind of France.

This identification was further strengthened in the early years of the twentieth century, when city and cathedral were mercilessly bombarded in World War I. After the terrible battles of the Marne and the Aisne, the cathedral, battered almost beyond recognition, nevertheless still stood—"blackened, wrapped in mourning like a mother who has seen her children perish," as one French soldier wrote in a tiny pocket diary. He had crawled among grapevines on a hillside beyond the city when he came upon his first distant view of the cathedral. The diary continued: "She makes me understand what I am doing. She is the image of what we are defending in France."

VI

The Rebeginning

W orld War I, involving most of the nations of Europe, the Middle East, the United States, Russia, and Japan, was the biggest armed conflict the world had known up to the day when the opening shots were fired by the German Army. The incident which touched it off—the assassination of an Austrian archduke—was an excuse to put into action battle plans which had been laid for more than a year. The war sprang from deep roots of European nationalism. Each nation had been ruthlessly pursuing individual goals, regardless of the impact on its neighbors.

The fighting was only one month and one day old when, on September 4, 1914, the Germans marched into Reims. At nine-thirty in the morning, Remois heard three distinct explosions. Shopkeepers, housewives rushed into the streets to exchange theories on the cause. "The Germans are blowing up railroad bridges," said one.

"No," said another, "they are firing a salvo to celebrate the entry they are about to make."

"That's not cannon fire," observed a third. "It's shelling."*

---

* The conversation is excerpted from the diary of a Remois nurse, Alice Martin, published by Gabriel Beauchesne, Libraire-Éditeur, Paris, 1914, as *Sous les Obus et dans les Caves: Notes d'une Bombardée de Reims.*

Seconds later a long strident whistle shrilled through the air, followed almost immediately by a thunderous explosion. The streets emptied faster than they had filled. Doors slammed. Inside, people dived under beds, tables, counters— the nearest shelter. There they stayed for three quarters of an hour while 380 projectiles were fired into the city, killing sixty people. When the Germans entered the town later in the day, they apologized. The bombardment, they said, had been a mistake. The Remois were dubious. They believed it had been meant to terrorize them.

Contrary to the fears of the Remois, the occupying force behaved in a most civil fashion. They secluded themselves in empty buildings and warehouses, emerging only to buy provisions. They paid the going prices for these without question. The white Remois sausage tucked in a roll of pastry found special favor with the German palate, and sausage merchants rejoiced in a spectacular business. For almost a week, the only reminder of war was a rumble of artillery from the south.

Then, on the tenth of September, eight hundred Germans, their flesh riddled with shrapnel, were brought to Reims. They filled all the hospitals. On the eleventh and twelfth more arrived, also carts and autobuses of wounded French. These were the victims of the battle of Épernay, eighteen miles south of Reims.

The cathedral was converted into a hospital, with the flag of the Red Cross hoisted to one of its tower tops. The occupying German force, ordered to leave Reims by the divisions of British and French who won the battle of Épernay, dug themselves into the surrounding slopes. In the cathedral, they left behind 130 of their wounded.

On one slope the Germans set up bombardment units. The first shell from these units fell in front of the cathedral at eight-fifteen on the night of September 17. It killed a beggar who customarily sat there at evening prayer time. Death froze the corpse, cross-legged, hand outstretched.

Intermittent shelling continued through the next day and night. At seven forty-five on the morning of the nineteenth, the real passion of the cathedral of Reims began. In twelve hours, five hundred fire bombs were aimed at it. Thirty of them scored direct hits.

The most devastating landed on a wooden scaffolding that surrounded the northwest tower. Workmen had erected it to repair previous damage. At four o'clock in the afternoon, when the bomb hit, the scaffolding caught fire. Crackling tongues of flame licked their way rapidly to wooden doors that opened on the galleries of the towers. The doors were fast consumed, and through the open spaces a strong east wind fanned the fire higher. The wooden sections of the roof went up in smoke; metal and lead dissolved. The town firemen were powerless. The Germans had bombed the water conduits.

A French aviator, Maurice Hollande, described the result from the perspective of the sky: "a . . . vision of an enormous cross of fire designed by the burning contours of nave and transepts, from the vaulted tops of which reddened smoke billowed like breath leaving a body."

Incandescent metal, raining down from the roof, set fire to

the straw on which the German wounded lay. The French had been evacuated. Screaming, the Germans tried to crawl through the inferno of smoke and flame to the relative safety of the square outside. The Mayor of Reims and clergy and Red Cross workers wrapped wet cloths around their heads and faces and groped their way into the cathedral. They dragged to safety all but fifteen of the 130 men. Those rescued were taken down to the cellars where champagne was fermented and stored by the wine merchants of Reims. More than half the city's population had sought refuge in these cellars. Most of the others had fled.

At seven in the evening the bombardment began to die down. A nurse, Alice Martin, described the scene: "The cathedral was standing but I didn't recognize it. The towers seemed taller, detached in purple smoke; below the towers a gaping chasm. There were some blunt needles I had never seen; these were the gables of the transept, detached from the embrace of the caved-in roof. And finally the apse, an incandescent cage where embers of the roof girders still glowed."

Alice went down to the cellars with the wounded. Her mother and sister were there. "My throat was so locked," she wrote in her diary, "it was all I could do to get out three words: 'The cathedral burns.' " She added: "My face, contorted, told them the rest. Tied together by our grief, at the bottom of the cellar the three of us wept silently." Later she explained, "One must be Remois to understand what feelings the words '*La Cathédrale*' evoke in us . . . . For us the cathedral is the soul of our city, it is the expression of

our common ideal, the recapitulation of all our history, the
heart of our religious life. Our forefathers all worked to
beautify and support it: a little bit of it belongs to each of
us. Where the cathedral is, is Reims, is home."

The next morning, September 20, in the still-smoldering
ruins, Mass was celebrated. It was the last Mass in the cathedral for thirteen years. Four more bombardments, on
September 22, September 24, October 12, and October 24,
from the air, left the stone skeleton too dangerous to occupy.

At that last Mass what did the Remois see as they filed
into their cathedral? At the center door of the main entrance,
Gabriel, indomitable, still grinned. Not so the angel who
greeted them at the left door. His body stood in place, but
his face was smashed. Later in the day masons hunted for bits
and pieces of that face. Guided by a mask from a museum,
they plastered it back together.

Little of the statuary escaped deformity. Molten lead
poured from the mouths of gargoyles and hardened like
stalactites hanging from their lips. Smiles turned to ghoulish
grimaces. "The statues," wrote Alice Martin in her diary,
"were . . . like the figures of the condemned on a gibbet,
or like the sheaths of skinless mummies. Behind them, in
places where blackened crusts of burned lead had scaled off
the walls, one saw great white stains, like leprosy."

The soldier who had defined the meaning of Reims in
his pocket journal made a new note: "On entering the city
I came directly to the cathedral . . . I gazed at the great
portal, scorched and carbonized by fire. The bombardment
had assassinated the saints, scalping St. Nicaise, as the bar-

barians had done." He recorded weeping at the ravage of the smiling angel—"that creature radiant with a celestial joy mortals cannot know." He mused that long before the great Italian Renaissance painter Leonardo da Vinci created the mysteriously smiling Mona Lisa, "some sculptor of this countryside gave an even more exalted mystery to this angel of stone . . ." In the end, the soldier took heart. He smiled back at Gabriel, believing enough of the cathedral was left to make reconstruction possible. "What miracle workers they were," he wrote, "these builders of the thirteenth century who made this masterpiece of architecture so solid that at the age of seven hundred years it has been able to take such an assault and yet remain standing!"

Looking up as they entered for that September Mass in 1914, the Remois saw a gaping hole where the great rose window had been. The panes were shattered, the lead between them melted. A group of firemen searched the ruins for chips and shards of the precious glass. They stored all they could find in a trunk, against the day when the window could be replaced. Other stained-glass windows were similarly damaged. People gathered the fragments as though they were jewels. Some actually set them in rings. Most of the cathedral treasure melted or burned in the inferno. The tapestries were ashes; so was a robe said to have belonged to St. Remi. His melted Communion cup and his bronze candlestick were indistinguishable from other molten metals. By some miracle, half the ornately carved choir stalls escaped harm. So did the organ and an intricate fourteenth-century clock adorned with figures of Mary, Joseph, and the three Wise Men who paraded with the striking of the hour. But these stood alone in mute witness to the glory that had been.

The steeples of the cathedral were toppled, and with them the bells—which broke from the fall, then melted. The first falling bell hit the bell ringer on the head, killing him instantly. No bells tolled for his funeral the following day.

Four of the flying buttresses were broken. The central pillars holding up the roof at the point where the nave and transepts met were nearly severed. Even before the bombardment ceased, masons shored up buttresses and pillars with bricks. Otherwise the whole building would have caved in then and there.

During recurring bombardments from the beginning of September until the end of October, the Remois lived mainly underground in the miles of champagne cellars which wound out to the hills. It was cold down there, but families brought blankets. It was dark, but they brought candles and spirit lamps. The latter they also used to heat food.

One girl organized a school. A minister held interdenominational services. Commented Alice Martin: "Whether Catholic or Protestant, one prayed well in the cellars. We became one family of one God."

Whenever someone ventured aboveground to replenish food supplies, the first question asked on his return was, "How is it with the cathedral? Does it still stand?" One day a man came back with a newspaper he had picked out of a gutter. In it were published international comments and condolences on the bombing. The paper was passed from hand to hand until it was tattered and worn beyond reading.

Toward the beginning of October, a time in France when long shafts of the autumn sun pour like mellow wine over valley and slope, people began to emerge from the cellars to lift their faces to the light. They talked while basking, noting daily changes in the foliage from green to yellow, and in the vineyards from red to purple. At the first distant sound of a bomb's whistle, they dived for the cellars again, "like rats for a hole," said Alice Martin. After a while they could distinguish by sound which bombs were German and which their own. The children became particularly skillful at making this distinction.

By mid-October the French and British had pushed the Germans back to a line about five miles west of Reims. What was left of the city—two thirds of it had been wiped out—was in Allied hands. But all through the war, severe fighting continued along a battle line known as the western front, part of which lay less than two miles away. It was impossible for the city to escape the consequences. Before the war ended in 1918, twenty-six more bombardments, mostly with fire bombs, all but leveled the remaining third of Reims. Only twenty houses were left standing. The last bombing, about a month before the signing of the armistice, was described in vivid notes by a Remois: "Houses where fire rages within are like intact carcasses . . . their windows violently lighted, their flaming curtains floating outside. One would think the devil was holding a party."

The armistice finally brought an end to the inferno. On

November 11, 1918, it was signed aboard the train of the French commander, Marshal Foch, in the forest of Compiègne, some fifty miles northwest of Reims. Shortly afterward the Croix de Guerre and the Légion d'honneur, both with palm-spray insignia attached, were awarded to the city of Reims for "most magnificent courage." These highest of French military honors were pinned to Reims's coat of arms. They are displayed today in a glass case in the city hall.

Almost immediately after the war, reconstruction of the devastated cathedral began. In the early nineteen-twenties, a great push came from America when the philanthropist John D. Rockefeller, Jr., gave the French government more than half a million dollars for rebuilding the roof and towers. The government raised the money for the rest of the job and assigned its Architect in Charge of Historic Monuments to direct the work. The architect's name was Henri Deneux, and for twenty years the cathedral was his life.

A passionate student of medieval art, Deneux was a worthy successor to all who had labored before him. The result of his endeavors is the peach-colored reconstruction of the plans of his predecessors one sees today. At the time Deneux began his colossal task, a profusely illustrated history of the cathedral from the thirteenth to the twentieth century was published for the young French. The history is presented as the dream of a wounded soldier of World War I. One of the smiling angels comes to the soldier in this dream and tells him the story of the cathedral's life. When the soldier asks who the angel is, he receives this reply: "I am the spirit of the cathedral. I am always young. The story of my life is the most glorious and the most poetic of all stories. I am all the history of France. I *am* France."

This was the young, the glorious, the poetic spirit that Henri Deneux sought to raise from rubble as day by day, stone by stone, repair mounted on repair. First, all the rubble was gathered and cleaned for reuse. The salvage was inspired not merely by a sense of thrift but by sentiment. These crumbled stones wore history's halos. Chips were molded into blocks. Hunks were pressed directly into the walls. Broken columns were filled with cement and plastered over. The final structural step was the new Rockefeller roof. It, too, was cement. Deneux was taking no more chances with inflammable roofs. But to keep the new one in harmony with the medieval style he was re-creating, he had the cement mixed and poured as it had been in the Middle Ages—by hand.

To replace the stained glass Deneux chose Jacques Simon, a descendant of the Paul Simon who had repaired the windows under Viollet-le-Duc. Jacques knew—and was able to duplicate—the process his forebear had used to create the medieval look. In addition, he had the passion of a Gaucher de Reims for reflecting local countryside and rural occupations. His windows were perfect accompaniments for reconstructions of Gaucher's friezes and column heads. One set of the Simon windows deals with wine making, long a Remois specialty, and by Jacques Simon's time the main source of income—in the form of champagne production—for seventy-five percent of the people.

Simon's panorama shows laborers tending the vineyards, harvesting and pressing grapes, and distilling the mash to wine. Against a startling sapphire background he outlines steeples of neighboring villages, spelling out the names of the vineyards and wine cellars possessed by each. From the sidelines, figures of St. Vincent, the patron adopted by vineyard workers, and John the Baptist, patron chosen by wine-cellar workers, gaze approvingly on the busy scenes. To another side, Christ, attending the wedding in Cana where the host ran out of wine, works the miracle of turning water into wine. At the summit, above all these, is the mystic winepress, much as it is seen on the painted linen cloth in the collection of those medieval Remois hangings now housed in the Reims Museum of Fine Arts.

Not until 1954 was the replacement of all the stained glass complete. From 1939 to 1945, the work was interrupted by World War II. During the greater part of that war, France was ruled and the northern half occupied by Hitler's Nazis, who set out to conquer the world. In the opening months of World War II, Hitler succeeded in gaining control of much of Western Europe.

In the conquered European countries as well as in Germany, citizens who opposed Hitler formed underground organizations to sabotage his plans. Guerrilla fighters blew up stores of ammunition, disrupted railroad lines, collected valuable information, and turned it over to British, American, and other armies fighting to defeat the dictator.

In France, which was among the conquered countries, the underground was known as the *Maquis*. The name first came from a tightly tangled bush which covers the French island of Corsica. Then, long ago, it was taken over by gangs of bandits, rebels, and outlaws who hid out in that bush. Finally the French World War II underground inherited the name. In the vicinity of Reims, almost two thousand Maquis operated. They dynamited the locks on river canals. They chopped down the poles between which electricity lines were strung. They killed or captured 1,700 Nazi soldiers. For these acts of sabotage they paid dearly. Only 298 survived the war. Some were deported to Germany, where they died or were killed in Nazi concentration camps. Others were massacred in France or killed in combat.

Among those who gave their lives was Father Antoine Lamouroux, a priest of the cathedral of Reims. He was the leader of a Maquis cell whose main task was sheltering Jews and activist anti-Nazis who had fled from Germany and the lands Hitler had conquered. To shelter such refugees Father Lamouroux and his co-conspirators constructed a secret chamber in one of the champagne cellars. The entrance, which also served as exit, was a narrow tunnel carved through a hillside. It was just big enough for a person to wiggle through like a snake. The hillside opening was camouflaged with turf and stones. Inside the chamber, Father Lamouroux's cell hid victims of Nazi persecution until such time as escapes could be arranged. Here, too, they forged the identity cards and passports with which they often had to furnish the refugees.

The main escape routes over which the fugitives were helped to reach England or Sweden were three: one led via the Vesle, Aisne, Oise, and Seine Rivers and connecting canals to Le Havre and the sea. A second wound from the Oise northward to the Somme and the small port of Saint-Valéry-sur-Somme. A third plied farther north along the Canal du Nord and the tiny river Aa to Gravelines on the English Channel. An elaborate network of fishing boats, river barges, and rowboats, all belonging to the Maquis, transported the escapees as stowaways or disguised as crew.

After making their getaways, many of these people joined one of the armies fighting Hitler. Some, especially those from Germany, were able to give valuable information to the governments of countries trying to stop him. Numerous Germans made frequent trips back to Germany, operating as spies for the British and Americans. It was a dangerous business. Not all those who tried to escape made it. Not all those who helped them survived.

Father Lamouroux's last mission was, for him, one of the unlucky ones. At midnight on April 4, 1943, he stood on the bank of the Vesle River, where it flows past the tiny village of Fismes, about six miles out of Reims. In a small bag he carried articles needed for Communion. Sewed with the tiniest of stitches into various places in the thick wool lining of his cape, he carried forged travel documents. A cold drizzle was falling. The night, moonless and starless, was bleak. The flat-bottomed boat for which he was waiting was late. The rowers had learned not to splash water, but so practiced were the priest's ears that he could recognize the plop-plop of dripping droplets as the oars were lifted smoothly, vertically, from the river.

There was no plop. Instead, footsteps behind him. Hands gripped his shoulders, wheeled him around. A member of the Gestapo, one of the Nazi secret police, held him fast. A second grabbed his satchel and opened it. The Communion vessels tumbled out. The Nazi tossed the satchel to the ground. Then he helped his companion strip the priest. They searched his clothes and body, found nothing.

"What are you doing here?" asked the first man in broken French.

"I took Communion to one who is dying there," Father Lamouroux replied, gesturing toward the village. "Now I am waiting for a friend to take me back to the city."

"Who dies?" demanded the questioner.

"A young girl, Rose Verrière."

"It is true," said the Nazi to his companion in German. "He says he has been with a dying girl. I know the family." He motioned to the shivering priest to reclothe himself. Barely had Father Lamouroux dressed when he heard the plop. The Nazis must be lured from the riverbank before the boat arrived. Leaving his cape on the ground so that the precious documents could be found, he picked up his satchel and threw it in the face of one of the Nazis, at the same time delivering a kick in the groin to the other. Then he took to his heels.

In an instant they were after him. One drew his pistol and fired as he ran. The shot missed. The priest paused. The approaching boatload would have heard the shot and halted. The Nazis caught up with the priest, tied his hands behind his back, and led him to the village center. Four days later he was deported to Buchenwald, one of the Nazi concentration camps. He never returned.

Displayed in Reims city hall, along with the honors awarded after World War I, is the Croix de Guerre with palm spray presented to the city at the end of World War II. It was won by the bravery of such men as Father Lamouroux, as well as by the courage of the Remois in the early days of the war when the city had again been besieged by advancing troops from Germany.

The end of the war in Europe came on the seventh of May 1945. Very early on that date, General Oberst Jodl and Admiral von Friedeberg signed Germany's unconditional surrender. The surrender took place in the classroom of a small red-brick schoolhouse in Reims; the time was two forty-one on a misty morning. Seated around a long wooden table were the two German officers, ten British and American commanders, and a general of the Free French Forces, which had been organized in Africa. The red schoolhouse has since been turned into a museum. On the walls of the historic classroom, war maps mark the tides of World War II. In the corridor outside hang pictures of the local Maquis heroes who, like Father Lamouroux, helped push back the rolling advance of Europe's would-be Nazi conquerors.

And today? Is the spirit that has strengthened the wills of so many generations of Remois still alive and well in the cathedral of Reims? It is, and as it has ever been, in a fashion that complements the life style of the current generation. The girl in the yellow pants suit and the boy in the blue jeans who may collect the offering at a cathedral service these days are members of a Catholic Action Group for the young French which the cathedral sponsors. Among the group's concerns: circumstances which justify refusal to serve in the army; employment and career opportunities for youth; problems of unmarried mothers. As the name of the group implies, members take action to try to solve problems.

For younger boys and girls the cathedral sponsors or shelters Scouts, Pioneers, and a half dozen other educational and recreational associations. For parents there are study-research-action projects focused on such dilemmas as locating or creating day care for the pre-school children of working fathers and mothers; surveying housing facilities—an ever-present problem in all urban France; and studying ways and means to expand them.

Looking at a few issues of *Reims-Notre Dame,* the cathedral's monthly bulletin, gives a wide-lens picture of its interests. The bulletin reviews books, stereo records, television programs. It gives advice on child-rearing, safe driving, marriage, and vacation trips. Feature articles cover a wide range of subjects, for instance, housing and employment needs of the some nine thousand foreign residents of Reims, the majority of them vineyard laborers and household helpers from Spain and North Africa. In the same issue is an analysis of the income and budget of the city of Reims, also tips to parents on how to help children with reading difficulties. There are frequent commentaries on conservation of natural resources, problems of the aged, trends in the public schools, urban renewal. Varied as the headlines are, they have a common root: response to challenge. Or, as Monsignor Berton, Reims's 156th archbishop, liked to say, "God in action." Not a new idea for the cathedral of Reims.

In September 1971, when Reims held the annual festival with which it honors St. Remi, Monsignor Berton marched through the streets with Archbishop Zourngana of Ouagadougou, Upper Volta, a former French colony in West Africa. Priests carrying crosses preceded them, as they had preceded St. Remi and Clovis on that day almost fifteen hundred years before when the saint had marched Clovis to the cathedral for baptism. But aside from the priests, the chanting choirs and reverent crowds, there were no reminders of old traditions—no canopy of veils above, no velvet carpet underfoot—none of the panoply with which Clovis and his successors surrounded such occasions. Come fire or revolution, come bombs or bloodshed, the cathedral has never succumbed to seeking contentment in long-gone glories. As if it possessed a clock with hands that always read *now* and with chimes that forever toll *tomorrow*, Reims rests on history while making it.

At the altar that September day, the two archbishops celebrating Mass together symbolized modern France as surely as Remi and Clovis symbolized the nation's founding or Joan of Arc its unifying. Upper Volta, Archbishop Zourngana's homeland, is one of eighteen important West African countries which, with the Indian Ocean island of Madagascar, are known as Afrique Noire Francophone, French-Speaking Black Africa. The seventeen on the mainland cover more than half the continent. The eighteen account for close to a third of Africa's total population. Once France ruled almost all of them. Now they are independent states. As such, each has signed economic, cultural, and defense agreements with France, creating partnerships between sovereign governments.

Against the background of this partnership, Archbishops Berton and Zourngana feted St. Remi. As they descended the sanctuary steps to offer Communion to the congregation, a shaft of sunlight, piercing prisms of the rose window, broke up into reflections of rainbow color on the floor at their feet. A small child on his mother's lap in the front row reached toward the patch, gurgling with delight.

Outside, the steadfast angels smiled.

BIBLIOGRAPHY

Aubert, Marcel, Campagnes de Construction de la Cathédrale de Reims. Académie des Inscriptions et Belles-Lettres (April–June 1943). Pub. by Henri Didier, Paris.

Baudrillat, Monseigneur de L'Académie Française, *Le Sacre de Charles VII et le Triomphe de Jeanne d'Arc, Discours Prononcé dans la Cathédrale de Reims à l'Occasion du Cinquième Centenaire, le 17 Juillet 1929.* Paris: SRÈS, 1929.

Bouchez, L'Abbé Émile, *Le Clergé du Pays Rémois pendant la Revolution et la Suppression de l'Archevêché de Reims, de 1789 à 1821.* Reims: Lucien Moore, 1912.

Boussinesa, Georges, Laurent, et Gustave, *Histoire de Reims Depuis les Origines Jusqu'au Nos Jours.* Reims: Matol-Braine, 1933.

Bruignac, Duroy de, "La Cathédrale de Reims dans la Vie Populaire et devant la Science." *Travaux de l'Académie Nationale de Reims,* July 1938.

Burnard, R., and Benito, E. G., *Reims, Septs Siècles d'Histoire devant la Cathédrale.* Paris-Nancy: Berger-Levrault, 1918.

Colombies, Pierre de, *Les Chantiers des Cathédrales.* Paris: A. & J. Picard et Cie, 1953.

Coqualt, Pierre, *Histoire de l'Eglise, Ville et Province de Reims Contenant Ses Douze Evechés Suffragenées avec le Rapport de Toutz les Concilz Tenuz en la Chrestianté des Papes.* Bibliothèque de Reims, Cabinet des Manuscrits, Nos. 1607–1613.

Cram, Ralph Adams, *La Cathédrale de Reims, Hier, Aujourd'hui, Demain*. Boston: Marshall Jones, 1918.

Crouvezier, G., *La Cathédrale de Reims*. Paris: Nouvelles Éditions Latines, 1971.

Debussy, Claude, *La Cathédrale Engloutie*. Angel Records #35066, in *Preludes*, Book I. Played by Walter Gieseking.

Demaison, Louis, "Les Architectes de la Cathédrale de Reims." *Bulletin Archéologique*, Paris, 1890.

——, "Reims à la Fin du XII Siècle." *Travaux de L'Académie Nationale de Paris*, Vol. 139 (1924–5).

——, "Les Cathédrales de Reims antérieures au XIII Siècle." *Bulletin Monumental*, Vol. 8 (1926).

——, *Une Monographie de la Cathédrale*. Collection des Petites Monographies des Grands Édifices, M. LaFèvre Pontalis, Paris, 1925.

——, "Topographie de Reims en 1228, d'Après le Registre de la taille du Sacre de Philippe VI." *Travaux de l'Académie Nationale de Reims*, Vol. 141 (1926–7).

Deneux, Henri, "Des Modifications Apportées à la Cathédrale de Reims au Cours de Sa Construction du XIII–XV Siècle." *Bulletin Monumental*, Vol. 166 (1948).

——, *Le Clocher à l'Ange de la Cathédrale de Reims*. Les Monuments Historiques de la France, Bul. de la Commission des Monuments Historiques, Paris (July 1936).

——, "La Restauration de la Cathédrale de Reims." *Construction Moderne*, Années 54 et 70.

Eschapasse, Maurice, *La Cathédrale de Reims*. Paris: Caisse Nationale des Monuments Historiques, 1971.

Feray, Jean. "Reims Palais du Tau, ancien Archevêche." Tiré de la revue *Connaissance des Arts*, No. 245, July 1972.

Flodoard, *Historia Remensis Ecclesiae* (*Histoire de l'Église de Reims*), trans. by F. Clément. Reims: Libraire-Éditeur Gruache, 1854.

Gilet, Louis, *La Cathédrale Vivante*. Paris: Flammarion, 1964.

Gilman, Laurence, "Claude Debussy, Poet and Dreamer." *North American Review*, Vol. 183 (October–December 1906).

Hollande, Maurice, *La Passion de Notre Dame de France*. Paris: Laffont, 1923.

Honnecourt, Villard de, *L'Album de Villard de Honnecourt*. Bibliothèque Nationale, MS 1726-A.

Hugo, Victor, "Guerre aux Démolisseurs." *Revues de Deux Mondes* (Mars 1832).

——, "Le Sacre de Charles X," *Odes et Morceaux Choisis de Victor Hugo*. Paris: Fasquelles, 1898.

Jadart, Henri, "Jeanne d'Arc à Reims." *Travaux de l'Académie Nationale de Reims*, Vol. 136 (1923).

——, "Journal d'un Rémois." Les Champs de Bataille, "Les Cités Meurtries," 1914–1915, *Travaux de l'Académie Nationale de Reims*, Vol. 137 (1924).

——, "Les Passages et Séjours de Henri IV à Reims en 1606." *Travaux de l'Académie Nationale de Reims*, Vol. 134 (1921).

Kalas, Ernest, "Les Aspects de la Ville de Reims à la Veille de l'Armistice." *Travaux de l'Académie Nationale de Reims*, Vol. 137 (1924).

Kurth, Godefroi, *Saint Clotilda*. London: Duckworth, 1906.

Le Sacre et Couronnement de Louis XIV, Roy de France et de Navarre dans l'Eglise de Reims, le Septième Juin, 1654. Paris: Chez Jacques Chardon, avec approbation et privilège du Roi; original imprimé chez Nicolas Hannisset, Soissons, 1694.

Levillain, L., "Le Baptème de Clovis." *Revue d'Érudition de la Bibliothèque de l'École de Chartes*, Vol. LXVII (1906).

Lille, Victor Canet, *Clovis et Les Origines de la France*. Société de Saint Augustin, 1887.

Martin, Alice, *Sous les Obus et dans les Caves: Notes d'une Bombardée de Reims*. Paris: Gabriel Beauchesne, 1914.

Mély, F. de. "Nos Vieilles Cathédrales et Leurs Maîtres." *Revues Archéologiques,* Vols. 11 and 13, Paris (1920).

Phillips, C. H., "The Symbolists and Debussy." *Humberside,* Vol. VIII, no. 5 (1930).

Pillion, Louise L., *Les Sculpteurs de Reims.* Paris: Rieder, 1928.

——, *Maîtres d'Oeuvre et Tailleurs de Pierre des Cathédrales.* Paris: Robert Laffont, 1947.

Poiries, Jules, *Reims, 1 Août à 31 Décembre 1914.* Librairie Payot, 1917.

Poncheville, André M. de., "La Cathédrale de Reims, Vue par un Soldat de la Marne." *La Revue Critique des Idées et des Lettres,* Vol. 29 #172 (September 1920).

"Rapport Officiel de la Bombardement de la Cathédrale de Reims." *Arts et Artistes,* Vol. 20, Paris (1915).

Registre des Actes Émanés de la Juridiction Volontaire des Échevins. Archives de Reims 1406–12, fol. 45r et 75 v.

Reims-Notre Dame, issues September 1971–November 1972.

Rogier, Jean, *Mémoires sur l'Histoire de Reims Depuis la Fin du XII Siècle.* Bibliothèque de Reims, Cabinet de Manuscrits, Nos. 1627–39.

Tarpel, Guillaume, *Reims, Cathédrale Nationale.* Paris: L'Office de la Centralisation d'Ouvrages, 1939.

Tientôt, Yvonne, *Debussy, l'Homme, Son Oeuvre, Son Milieu.* Henri Lemoine et Cie., 1962.

Vervaeck, L., "La Découverte du Tombeau de St. Albert de Louvain." *Annalecta Bollandiana,* Vol. xlv (1922).

INDEX